In the Garden of Our Lord

RICKY CLEMONS

PUBLISHED BY FIEDLI PUBLISHING, INC.

Copyright ©2021, Ricky Clemons
ALL RIGHTS RESERVED.

No part of this publication may be reproduced, stored in a retrieval system, or transmitted in any form or by any means—electronic, mechanical, photo-copy, recording, or any other—except for brief quotation in reviews, without the prior permission of the author or publisher.

ISBN: 978-1-60414-621-9

Published by

Fideli Publishing, Inc.
119 W. Morgan St.
Martinsville, IN 46151
www.FideliPublishing.com

Table of Contents

The Garden of Our Faith 1

In the Garden of the Lord 3

We are Imperfect People 5

It's Easy to Sin Against You, O Lord 7

It is a Great Day 9

Oh, What One Man Can Do 11

The Sound of Spiritual Food 13

If You and I Know Better 15

On the Holy Sabbath Day of Rest 17

I Am Unclean, Filthy, and Dirty with Sin 19

What I Know About Jesus Christ 21

All of Our Spiritual Brothers and Sisters 23

You Can Want Things to Be Perfect 25

It's Your Holy Spirit 27

If It Was True 29

The Lord has to Drag Us Out 31

Age Older 33

Rejecting the Lord 35

Will Allow Us to See 36

A Heavy Blow 38

Our Trials Can't Stop 40

It's No Excuse 42

The Devil's Mind-Control Techniques 44
The Devil Has His Human Agents 46
Many People Live By.. 48
The Lord Can Prepare Us 50
I Wrestled with the Lord.. 52
Love Is Not 54
Jesus Christ, Our Lord, Is the Living Truth 56
Owe Them Something 58
Problems... 60
The Pathway 62
Choices.. 63
Knowledge.. 65
Within You 67
Can't Put Our Trust in Tomorrow.. 69
Love to Use People 71
Stories.. 73
God is Fair 74
To Make it to Heaven 76
We Should Not Let Temporary Things... 78
Don't Be Ashamed... 80
Fault... 82
The Lord Will Test Our Love 84
The Unknown 86
Do Not Weigh More.. 88

You are Alive	90
I Love My Church Family	92
Going Through Trials	94
We Worship a Holy God	96
Not Waiting on the Lord	98
More and More	100
Are Only a Dream	102
We Shouldn't Love to Point Our Fingers	103
The Greatest Test Of Our Faith	105
We Need To	107
Cities Are Made Up Of	109
Don't Get Our Way	111
Loves Everybody the Same	113
If You Think on the Lord	115
That I Know	117
Will Not Go to Heaven	118
Close His Probationon this World	120
I Want to do Your Will, O Lord	122
Will Hurt Our Hearts	123
Medicine Can't Cure the Sin-Sick Soul	124
No One is More	125
You Can Always Talk to Jesus	126
We are Not Going Anywhere	127

The Garden of Our Faith

The garden of our faith in the Lord is a beautiful garden to the Lord.

It is a garden that only the Lord can always take good care of every day.

The garden of our faith in the Lord will grow God's favor upon you and me.

The Lord gives us forgiveness to grow in the garden of our faith in Him.

The Lord gives us knowledge of His holy word to grow in the garden of our faith in Him.

The Lord gives us love to grow in the garden of our faith in Him.

The Lord gives us joy to grow in the garden of our faith in Him.

The Lord gives us wisdom to grow in the garden of our faith in Him.

The Lord gives us endurance to grow in the garden of our faith in Him.

The Lord gives us contentment to grow in the garden of our faith in Him.

The Lord gives us patience to grow in the garden of our faith in Him.

The Lord gives us temperance to grow in the garden of our faith in Him.

The Lord gives us righteousness to grow in the garden of our faith in Him.

The Lord gives us holiness to grow in the garden of our faith in Him.

The Lord gives us experience to grow in the garden of our faith in Him.

The Lord gives us understanding to grow in the garden of our faith in Him.

The Lord gives us courage to grow in the garden of our faith in Him.

The Lord gives us perseverance to grow in the garden of our faith in Him.

The Lord gives us reverence to grow in the garden of our faith in Him.

The Lord gives us strength to grow in the garden of our faith in Him.

The Lord gives us discernment to grow in the garden of our faith in Him.

The Lord gives us a renewed mind to grow in the garden of our faith in Him.

The Lord gives us compassion to grow in the garden of our faith in Him.

The Lord gives us works to grow in the garden of our faith in Him.

The Lord gives us trials to grow in the garden of our faith in Him.

You and I will grow spiritual harvest crops in the garden of our faith in the Lord Jesus Christ.

All of our spiritual crops will never rot and dry up in the garden of our faith in the Lord, who is our ultimate spiritual farmer to harvest the crop of our souls into heaven when He comes back again.

In the Garden of the Lord

In the garden of the Lord there are no insects of disobedience.

In the garden of the Lord there are no pesticides of unrighteousness.

In the garden of the Lord there are no rotten sweet potatoes of greed.

In the garden of the Lord there are no rotten butter beans of lust.

In the garden of the Lord there are no rotten string beans of jealousy.

In the garden of the Lord there are no rotten lettuce of lies.

In the garden of the Lord there are no rotten carrots of unnatural affections.

In the garden of the Lord there are no rotten white potatoes of pride.

In the garden of the Lord there are no rotten collard greens of inequality.

In the garden of the Lord there are no rotten salad of prejudice.

In the garden of the Lord there are no rotten peas of injustice.

In the garden of the Lord there are no rotten tomatoes of deception.

In the garden of the Lord there are no rotten cabbages of fornication.

And the garden of the Lord there are no rotten beets of adultery.

In the garden of the Lord there are no rotten spinach of discrimination.

In the garden of the Lord there are no rotten kale of showing respect of persons.

In the garden of the Lord there are no rotten asparagus of discontent.

In the garden of the Lord there are no rotten corn of theft.

In the garden of the Lord there is no rotten broccoli of rebellion.

In the garden of the Lord there are no rotten Brussels sprouts of selfishness.

In the garden of the Lord there are no rotten red peppers of violence.

In the garden of the Lord there are no rotten green peppers of segregation.

In the garden of the Lord there are no rotten pinto beans of hate.

In the garden of the Lord there are no rotten radishes of lawlessness.

All of the Lord's vegetables are always ripe to pick in His beautiful garden.

The Lord will always invite you and me into His garden every day, and the Lord will give us His vegetables free of charge.

All of the Lord's vegetables are righteous to eat.

All of the Lord's vegetables are holy to eat.

All of the Lord's vegetables have no sins to ever rot.

We can always go in the Lord's garden and pick out His fresh vegetables that we will never have to cook and season for them to taste good to us.

The vegetables of this world are always rotten to the core.

Every day, so many people are eating the rotten vegetables of this world and getting spiritually sick, then vomiting it up and licking it back up like a dog licking up its vomit.

We are Imperfect People

We are imperfect people who can worship a perfect Lord and Savior, Jesus Christ.

Every day, many people love to talk about imperfect people.

Many people love to worship imperfect people.

In the Bible, there were imperfect people — except one person who was perfect.

That perfect man was Jesus Christ, who had no sins.

Many people today love to idolize imperfect people.

We Christians are imperfect people who love to worship and obey a perfect Lord and Savior, Jesus Christ.

We can be made perfect in God's eyesight through the righteousness of Jesus Christ.

It doesn't mean that we are perfect without ever having to confess and repent of our sins ever again.

For as long as we live in our sinful body, we can surely sin against the Lord regardless of those past sins which we repented.

We are imperfect people who Jesus Christ our Lord can save from our sins.

Many people would rather talk about imperfect people than talk about a perfect Lord and Savior, Jesus Christ, who never said one wrong word when He lived here on earth.

Many people would rather talk about imperfect people than talk about a perfect Lord and Savior Jesus Christ, who never did anything wrong when He lived here on earth.

Many people will love imperfect people more than loving our perfect Lord and Savior, Jesus Christ.

Many people will obey imperfect people more than obeying our perfect Lord and Savior, Jesus Christ.

Many people would rather put imperfect people up on a pedestal than put a perfect Lord and Savior, Jesus Christ, up on a pedestal that Jesus is truly worthy of forever and ever.

We all have sinned and fallen short of the glory of God.

If we imperfect people confess and repent of our sins unto Jesus Christ, then God will look at us as if we are perfect through the righteousness of Jesus Christ.

The righteousness of Jesus Christ covers over our imperfect lives.

We are imperfect people to sin against God for as long as we live, because sanctification is a lifetime process for us.

We need to love and obey Jesus Christ, our Lord, who we need to pray to without ceasing because we are imperfect and can sin against Him on any day.

It's Easy to Sin Against You, O Lord

It's so easy to sin against you, O Lord, in my thoughts.

It doesn't take a lot for me to think bad thoughts.

It doesn't take a lot for me to think bad thoughts about someone else.

It doesn't take a lot for me to think bad thoughts about myself.

It doesn't take a lot for me to think prideful thoughts about myself.

It's so easy to sin against you, O Lord, in my thoughts.

It's so easy to sin against you, O Lord, in my words.

It doesn't take a lot for me to say some bad words.

It doesn't take a lot for me to say some bad words about someone else.

It doesn't take a lot for me to say some bad words about myself.

It doesn't take a lot for me to say some prideful words about myself.

It's so easy to sin against you, O Lord, in my words.

It's so easy to sin against you, O Lord, in my actions.

It doesn't take a lot for me to do something bad.

It doesn't take a lot for me to do something bad to somebody else.

It doesn't take a lot for me to do something bad to myself.

Oh Lord, I need you to help me to think good thoughts about someone else.

Oh Lord, I need you to help me to think good thoughts about myself.

Most of all, oh Lord, I need you to help me to think good thoughts about You, who I can't question if things go wrong in my life.

Oh Lord, I need you to help me to say good words about someone else.

Oh Lord, I need you to help me say good words about myself.

Oh Lord, I need you to help me to say good words about You, even if You do not answer all of my prayers.

Oh Lord, I need you to help me to do good in my actions.

Oh Lord, I need you to help me to do someone else right.

Oh Lord, I need you to help me to do myself right.

Oh Lord, I need you to help me to do You right, by keeping Your commandments even if You allowed me to get sick to serve Your holy purpose.

It's so easy to sin against You, O Lord, who can cleanse me of my sins and can save me from being lost in my sins that I need to confess and repent unto You.

It is a Great Day

It is a great day for a couple to get married.

It is a great day for someone to start a business.

It is a great day for a prisoner to get out of prison.

It is a great day for lawyers to win their cases.

It is a great day for a mother to give birth to her baby.

It is a great day for someone to buy a house.

It is a great day for someone to buy a car.

It is a great day for someone to buy a truck.

It is a great day for someone to get a job.

It is a great day for someone to get a loan.

It is a great day for someone to get well.

It is a great day for someone to win the lottery.

It is a great day for college students to graduate from college.

It is a great day to be elected president of the United States.

It is a great day for someone who lived through a terrible car accident.

It is a great day to save someone's life.

It is a great day to win a war.

It is a great day for someone to graduate from high school.

It is a great day for someone to get an award.

It is a great day for someone to be found after getting lost.

It is a great day.

It is a great day for someone to wake up from a coma.

It is a great day for the doctor to tell someone that he or she is cancer free.

It is a great day for someone to get baptized in the church.

It is a great day for someone to give his or her life to the Lord.

It is a great day for someone to confess and repent of his or her sins unto the Lord.

It's a great day for someone to win souls to the Lord.

It will be a great day when Jesus Christ comes back again.

It will be a great day to go with Jesus back to heaven with all the Saints and with all of the holy angels.

Oh, What One Man Can Do

One man has caused all men to have a sinful nature and fall short of the glory of God.

One man can build up a nation and make it great.

One man can bring down a nation into ruins.

One man can start a war.

One man can end a war.

One man can start a riot.

One man can end a riot.

Oh, what one man can do.

One man can change the whole world.

There was one sinless man who died for the sins of all men.

There was one sinless man who got the victory over death and the grave.

There was one sinless man who is the Son of God.

There was one sinless man who forgave men of their sins.

There was one sinless man who can save all men from their sins.

There was one sinless man who rose from the grave and went back to heaven.

That one sinless man was Jesus Christ, who is the Son of God.

That one sinless man was Jesus Christ, who was the second Adam who never sinned against His Father, God.

That one sinless man was Jesus Christ, who is coming back again to give eternal life to all those saved in Him.

That one's sinless man was Jesus Christ who shed His precious blood on the cross and became sin on the cross to save you and me from being lost in our sins.

That one sinless man was Jesus Christ, who is representing our case in the heavenly courtroom of God.

Oh, what one man can do.

One man can save so many people from death.

That one man without sin was Jesus Christ, who can save anyone from eternal death for believing in Him.

One man can deceive so many people.

That one man without sin was Jesus Christ, who is the living truth to set all men free from lies and deceptions.

That one man without sin was Jesus Christ, who lived in this world to show sinful men who God is and what God requires from them.

That one man without sin was Jesus Christ, who all men can believe in and be saved from eternal death.

The Sound of Spiritual Food

Your dog will know the sound of food when you open the refrigerator door.

That door opening makes a sound your dog hears, and he sees you take some food out of your refrigerator.

Your dog will know the sound of food when you take the lid off of a bowl or tray.

Your dog will hear that sound and see you take some food out of the bowl or tray.

Your dog will know the sound of food when you eat your food and make a smacking sound.

Your dog will hear and see you swallow that food down.

Your dog will know the sound of food when you open the microwave door and put your food inside.

When your dog hears the microwave door close and sees you standing in front of the microwave he knows you're going to take out your plate of food.

You and I will know the sound of spiritual food when we hear the preacher's sermon about Jesus Christ, our Lord and Savior, who we can spiritually eat.

You and I will know the sound of spiritual food when the Bible school teacher opens the lesson and teaches it so we can hear and spiritually eat.

You and I will know the sound of spiritual food when someone gives a testimony about the Lord that we can hear and spiritually eat.

You and I will know the sound of spiritual food when we hear a gospel song and spiritually eat it.

You and I will know the sound of spiritual food when we hear someone pray for us and we can spiritually eat that prayer.

You and I will know the sound of spiritual food when we hear someone read the Bible scriptures and we will spiritually eat it.

A dog can hear the sound of food, but that doesn't mean that the dog can eat the food — you have to give the food to your dog.

It can be a different case with you and me, who will know the sound of spiritual food and can choose to eat that spiritual food on our own, without any help from someone else.

If You and I Know Better

If you and I know better to say what is right, we should say it to help others to say what is right too.

If you and I know better to do what is right, we should do what is right to help others to do what is right too.

We should always say what is right and always do what is right by what we know is right by the Lord.

If you and I know better to say what is right and don't say it, the Lord will hold us accountable for not saying what is right.

If you and I know better to do what is right and don't do it, the Lord will hold us accountable for not doing what is right.

Many people know better to say what is right, but they don't always say what is right.

Many people know better to do what is right, but they don't always do what is right.

Jesus Christ, the Lord, will hold you and me accountable if we know better and don't practice it day after day.

If you and I know better, especially by God's holy word, then we need to tell others what we know that is right in God's holy word.

When the Lord gives you and me the opportunity to share our belief in Him with others who just don't know better like you and me, then we should share our belief in Him with love and not with judgment.

There are many people who just don't know better and don't live right by God's holy word.

You and I must live right by example, and do it in their eyesight so they know better by what is right.

Knowing better to live right gives you and me no favor with God over those who don't know better.

God's favor can be upon those who don't know better when their heart is sincere with the Lord, even though they don't know better like you and I do.

If you and I know better to live right by the Lord, we must not hide that light under a bushel.

We must let our light shine before those who don't know better so they can know better after seeing you and me living right by the Lord.

On the Holy Sabbath Day of Rest

On the holy Sabbath day of rest, you can rest your mind from thinking on the daily routine of your thought processes.

On the holy Sabbath day of rest, you can rest your body from doing the daily routine of chores.

On the holy Sabbath day of rest, you can rest from all your work and can relax your mind and body to give all of yourself to Jesus Christ, the Lord of the Sabbath.

Jesus says that you can work for six days on your job.

You can work for six days doing your daily house chores.

You can work for six days operating your business.

You can work to make a living six days a week.

You can work to take care of your family six days a week.

Jesus did say that you can get the ox out of the ditch on the Sabbath.

That means you can help the sick to get well on the Sabbath.

Giving the Lord your time on the Sabbath can also be protecting your communities without wanting to get paid for doing it.

The Lord will not allow His children to beg for bread to eat.

The Lord will provide His blessings for you also on the Sabbath day of rest.

If someone's car is broken down on the road on the Sabbath, you can offer him or her a helping hand.

You can feed the hungry on the Sabbath.

You can do some good things in the name of the Lord on His holy Sabbath day of rest.

You shouldn't want to get paid for helping the sick to get well on the Sabbath.

The Lord will supply all of your needs, even on the holy Sabbath day of rest.

You can get the ox out of the ditch on the holy Sabbath day of rest, but you shouldn't want to get paid for doing it.

If you get paid for doing it, then you are working for man and not for the creator God.

The holy Sabbath day of rest is a Memorial Day of all God's creation that God rested from.

God did all of His works in six days when He created the heavens and the earth.

God rested on the seventh day of the week, being Saturday and not Sunday.

Jesus Christ said that He didn't come to change the law, but to fulfill the law.

Fulfilling the law is also keeping the Sabbath day holy unto the Lord.

You and I should give Him all of our time, from sunset Friday to sunset Saturday.

The Lord only commands twenty-four hours of our full time with Him, so He can bless us more abundantly in our mind, body, and soul.

Keeping the Sabbath is also getting the ox out of the ditch with no pay.

I Am Unclean, Filthy, and Dirty with Sin

I am unclean, filthy, and dirty with sin.

When it comes to the Lord Jesus Christ my righteousness is unclean, filthy, and dirty when it comes to the Lord.

Only the Lord's righteousness can cover my unclean, filthy and dirty righteousness.

The Lord's righteousness is forever and ever more purer than the pure white snowflakes falling from the sky.

Even in my dreams, I am unclean, filthy, and dirty with sin, for the Lord to wake me up out of my dreams that could kill me in my sleep if my Lord Jesus Christ didn't rescue me from my unclean and filthy dreams.

Every day, my righteousness is like filthy rags.

No one likes a filthy rag.

No one would want to wash their face with a filthy rag.

No one would want to bathe with a filthy rag.

No godly person and no wicked person would want to hold onto filthy rags.

No one in their right mind would want to carry around filthy rags.

Even the worst person in the world knows that filthy rags are not clean to use.

Only Jesus can clean you and me up with His blood that He shed on the cross for our sins.

Our sins are unclean, filthy, and dirty before a holy and righteous God.

Even our good works are unclean, filthy, and dirty without the Lord's blessing upon them.

No matter what good things that we do, we can't earn our way to be saved.

The Lord's salvation is forever more pure than gold and no one can ever afford to buy it.

The most wealthy people in this world have wealth that is unclean, filthy, and dirty before the Lord, whose eternal wealth is forever more pure than the purest water to drink.

I am unclean, filthy, and dirty with sin that I need to confess and repent of unto my Lord Jesus Christ, who's forever more pure than the clean air that I breathe.

What I Know About Jesus Christ

What I know about Jesus Christ is enough for me to believe in Jesus Christ.

I don't know all of the Bible scriptures about Jesus Christ, but I believe in Jesus Christ because of what I know about Him.

I don't have to know a lot of the Bible scriptures to believe in Jesus Christ, and no one can judge my belief in Jesus Christ.

Jesus knows my heart and that I believe in Him.

No one can judge my measure of belief in Jesus.

No one can say that my belief in Jesus Christ won't get stronger in my life.

No one knows how long Jesus will allow me to live, as my belief in Him continues to be like a high mountain.

What I know about my Lord and Savior Jesus Christ is enough for me to believe in Him each and every day.

I can't judge anyone else's belief in Jesus Christ, who is the only one that has the power to cleanse anyone of their sins.

Jesus knows who will always believe in Him and who will not always believe in Him.

Jesus knows what choices we will make before we make our choices.

You can look on my outward appearance and may want to judge my belief in Jesus Christ.

In your eyes, you may believe that I am playing church.

You just don't know how Jesus is cleansing my heart from the cholesterol of sin, when you are judging my belief in Jesus Christ.

Only the Lord Jesus Christ can judge my belief in Him, because He knows all of my thoughts and all that I feel, regardless of my outward works that I do in His holy name.

Jesus truly knows my motives and my intentions are true about believing in Him.

Regardless of what I say about Jesus Christ, He knows whether my belief in Him is great or small.

Jesus truly knows if I would give up my life for His holy name sake.

You can't judge my belief in Jesus Christ, when you don't truly know how your belief in Jesus Christ will be tested for you to pass or fail.

All of Our Spiritual Brothers and Sisters

One day, we will meet all of our spiritual brothers and sisters in the Lord, who will one day come back again on the clouds of glory.

We will all be so glad to see all of our spiritual brothers and sisters.

We will be so happy that they are saved in Jesus Christ, our Lord and Savior.

We all will hug and kiss one another with a holy hug and kiss on our cheeks.

We will weep with gladness to meet all of our spiritual brothers and sisters in the Lord.

We will sing happy songs about our Lord taking us back to heaven with Him and all the angels.

We will have so much joy in our hearts when we see all of our spiritual brothers and sisters.

We will be so amazed that we ourselves and our spiritual brothers and sisters made it over into the heavenly land of eternal life.

Most of all, we will be so happy to see our Lord and Savior Jesus Christ on the clouds of glory.

We will be so happy that He didn't forget us.

All of our spiritual brothers and sisters will make a joyful noise unto our Lord Jesus Christ.

We will be so happy to talk to all of our spiritual brothers and sisters.

We will have an eternity to get to know them all.

We will also meet and talk to our guardian angels, who will tell us how they protected us in so many ways that we can't ever count.

Most of all, we will get to talk to our Lord Jesus Christ face to face.

We will talk to Him, we will sing with Him, and we will laugh with Him.

We will also talk, sing, and laugh with all of our spiritual brothers and sisters in the Lord.

We will have forever and ever to learn more and more about our Lord Jesus Christ.

We will have forever and ever to learn more and more about the holy angels.

We will have forever and ever to learn more and more about all of our spiritual brothers and sisters.

We will have forever and ever to learn more and more about other worlds.

We will have forever and ever to learn more and more about all things that Jesus created for Himself.

We will be surprised to see some people who we believed to be lost in their sins, but we will be glad they repented and turned to the Lord, even in their last hour of being alive.

All of our spiritual brothers and sisters will be a number that no one can count except the Lord.

We will all be so happy to live forever and ever in the new heaven and new earth.

We will all be a holy and righteous people unto our Lord and Savior Jesus Christ.

I will be surprised and you will be surprised to go with Jesus back to heaven, because today we just don't know that we will make it into heaven.

Our good deeds can't entitle us to heaven.

We can believe that we will make it to heaven, but only the Lord truly knows for sure.

You Can Want Things to Be Perfect

You can want things to be perfect.

You can want to have a perfect business.

You can want to write a perfect book.

You can want to speak perfect words.

You can want to do everything perfect.

When you and I don't do everything perfectly, it can discourage us.

You can make a mistake and it can make you feel bad.

Someone else can make a mistake and it can have a bad effect on you, especially if your loved ones make a big mistake.

You can want to be perfect.

You can want your children to be perfect.

You can want your spouse to be perfect.

You can want to have a perfect career.

You can want to have a perfect profession.

You can want to have a perfect job.

You can rehearse things over and over again because you want it to be perfect.

You and I love to strive for perfection in what we do.

The Bible shows that perfection is always a good thing.

Perfection is from the Lord who is perfect without sin.

You and I have a sinful nature so we do not always do everything perfectly.

You and I have a sinful nature so we do not always speak perfect words.

You and I have a sinful nature so we do not always have perfect thoughts.

You and I want to be perfect because the Bible shows that from the beginning of God's creation everything was perfect.

Adam and Eve were perfect before they sinned against God.

The fallen angels were perfect before they sinned against God.

Being made perfect is only possible through the Lord.

You and I must be made perfect through the righteousness of Jesus Christ.

His righteousness is perfect.

Jesus does everything right all the time.

You and I don't do everything right all the time.

You and I can mean to do good and well to everybody, but we are not perfect in every word that we say and in every thing that we do.

Even an evil person loves perfection and wants to commit a perfect crime without getting caught.

You can want things in your life to be perfect, and there's nothing wrong with that as long as your life is about doing the Lord's perfect will.

Your will and my will are not perfect for us to fall short of the glory of God.

One day, we will be perfect without sin for being saved in Jesus Christ, who is coming back again to make us perfect to live in heaven where the holy angels are perfect.

It's Your Holy Spirit

It's Your Holy Spirit, O Lord, who softens my heart and brings tears to my eyes.

It's Your Holy Spirit, O Lord, who draws me more and more close to you my Lord and Savior Jesus Christ.

It's Your Holy Spirit, O Lord, who guards my soul to call out to you.

It's Your Holy Spirit, O Lord, who convicts me of the wrong words that I say.

It's Your Holy Spirit, O Lord, who convicts me of the wrong deeds that I do.

It's Your Holy Spirit, O Lord, who converts me to want to change for the better.

It's Your Holy Spirit, O Lord, who strengthens my mind to think thoughts about You and praise You for keeping me in my right mind.

It's Your Holy Spirit, O Lord, who leads me and guides me on Your straight and narrow road.

O, my Lord Jesus Christ, I thank you for Your Holy Spirit, who gives me the push that I need to keep my eyes on You, my Lord.

O, my Lord Jesus Christ, I thank you for giving me Your Holy Spirit to help me deny myself and pick up my cross and follow You, my Lord.

O, my Lord and Savior Jesus Christ, I thank You for giving me Your Holy Spirit to help me to love You and my neighbors.

O, Lord, it's Your Holy Spirit who shows me what a wretch I am without You in my life.

O, Lord, it's Your Holy Spirit who shows me that only You are worthy to be worshiped.

O, Lord, it's Your Holy Spirit who speaks the truth to me about You and about myself and my neighbors.

O, my Lord Jesus Christ, without Your Holy Spirit living in me, I would be better off having never been born in this world.

Without Your Holy Spirit, my Lord, there is no way that You would hear and answer my prayers.

If It Was True

If evolution was true, then God would have inspired His prophets and disciples to write about evolution being true.

The Bible says that God created the heavens and earth.

The Bible says that God created man and woman and all the animals.

If we could see the dead and speak to the dead, then God would have inspired His prophets and disciples to write about this being true.

The fallen angels can appear to us as our dead loved ones.

The fallen angels can speak to us and sound like our dead loved ones speaking to us.

The Bible says that the dead know nothing.

The Bible says that the dead can do nothing.

If it was true that we go to heaven right after we die, then God would have inspired His prophets and disciples to write about that being true.

Jesus Christ is coming back again to take us to heaven.

We can't go to heaven without Jesus taking us there when He comes back again.

If it was true that we have no sins, then God would have inspired His prophets and disciples to write about us having no sins.

Jesus Christ gave up His life for our sins.

He became sin on the cross in our place.

He rose from the grave with the victory over death and the grave.

He rose from the grave to save us from our sins.

If we have no sins, then we would never have to confess and repent of our sins.

We have sins to confess and repent of unto Jesus Christ.

Only Jesus had no sins when He lived on earth among sinners.

If it was true that there is no devil, then God would have inspired His prophets and disciples to write about that being true.

Sin is from the devil and evil is from the devil.

The Bible says that the devil is a liar, thief, and a murderer.

If it was true that there is no God, then nothing would exist — there would be no heaven, there would be no universe, and there would be no earth.

There would be no you and me.

There would be no visible things.

There would be no invisible things.

If a man says that there is no God, it is like saying that man does not exist.

The Lord has to Drag Us Out

The Lord has to drag us out of holding onto things that we don't need to hold onto.

The Lord has to drag us out of our old ways of doing things.

The Lord has to drag us out of our old grudges.

The Lord has to drag us out of our selfish ways.

The Lord had to drag Lot and his wife and two daughters out of Sodom and Gomorrah to save them from destruction, even though Lot's wife looked back and turned into a pillar of salt.

Even though the Lord has to drag us out of being lost in our sins, many people will turn around and look back on their selfish desires.

Many people will turn around and look back on their old ways of doing things.

Many people will turn around and look back on holding grudges.

Many people will turn around and look back on their selfish ways.

The Lord has to drag us out of things that are not good for us.

The Lord has to drag us out of making bad choices.

The Lord has to drag us out of our problems that we bring upon ourselves.

We can choose to not turn around and look back when the Lord drags us out of that old sinful way.

Because of our sinful nature, the Lord has to drag our minds out of thinking about anything that is not like Him.

Because of our sinful nature, the Lord has to drag us out of feeling ill towards anyone.

Because of our sinful nature, we can tend to want to hold onto our own right way of doing things.

Because of our sinful nature, we can tend to hold onto our own words to say. We can thank God for Jesus who has to drag us out of our pride.

The Lord has to drag us out of our comfort zone.

He is coming back again one day soon, and He doesn't want us to get relaxed in the ways of this sinful world.

Jesus has to drag us out of holding onto temporary things in this temporary world.

He wants us to hold onto Him, because He is eternal and will be around forever and ever.

Age Older

Many people will look younger than their age.

Many people will look older than their age.

The devil uses age for something bad.

As we age older, the devil uses age to show us wrinkles.

As we age older, the devil uses age to show us lack of energy.

As we age older, the devil uses age to show us brittle bones.

As we age older, the devil uses age to show us loss of memory.

The Lord uses age for something good, as we age older the Lord uses age to show us wisdom.

As we age older, the Lord uses age to show us experience.

As we age older, the Lord uses age to show us maturity.

As we age older, the Lord uses age to show us patience.

As we age older, the Lord uses age to show us humility.

Many people will age older and get more foolish.

Many people will age older and get more selfish.

Many people will age older and get more wicked.

Before Adam and Eve sinned against God, there was no age.

Age came into existence after Adam and Eve sinned against God.

Our days are numbered and we age older because of sin.

As long as we live, we will age older.

Every new day we age older.

Many people age older to be a father.

Many people age older to be a mother.

Many people age older to be an uncle.

Many people age older to be an aunt.

Many people age older to be a grandfather.

Many people age older to be a grandmother.

God in heaven has no age.

The angels have no age.

Even the animals will age older because of sin.

We can truly thank our Lord and Savior Jesus Christ for allowing us to age older in this sinful world.

The Lord doesn't allow sin to cause everyone to live a very short life, even though many people will shorten their own lives.

Even though age comes from sin, aging older is a blessing from the Lord.

Most people, if not all people, want to live until they get old because life is a very good thing.

The Lord wants to age us so we will hopefully be saved in Jesus Christ before we die.

Rejecting the Lord

Rejecting the Lord is like jumping off a boat in the middle of the ocean and having no life vest on.

Rejecting the Lord is like jumping out of an airplane without a parachute.

Rejecting the Lord is like walking into a poisonous snake on a dark night.

Rejecting the Lord is like walking into hot flames of fire.

Rejecting the Lord is like being buried alive.

Rejecting the Lord is like walking barefoot on broken glass.

Rejecting the Lord is like building a house with no foundation.

Rejecting the Lord is like cutting your own throat.

Rejecting the Lord is like drinking poison and knowing that it's poison.

Rejecting the Lord is like walking in front of a speeding truck.

Rejecting the Lord is like stabbing yourself with a sharp knife.

Rejecting the Lord is like cutting off your own leg.

Rejecting the Lord is like throwing acid on yourself.

Rejecting the Lord is like taking your own life.

Rejecting the Lord is like being all alone on a deserted island.

Rejecting the Lord is like walking through a minefield.

Rejecting the Lord is like losing your mind.

Rejecting the Lord is like a young inexperienced woman not knowing that she got in the car with a serial killer.

Rejecting the Lord is the worst thing that anyone can do.

Rejecting the Lord is like ruining your own life.

Rejecting the Lord is like a drunk man getting in a fight and getting knocked out, but when he wakes up he doesn't remember anything and then gets drunk again.

Will Allow Us to See

There are some things that the Lord will allow us to see.

There are some things that the Lord won't allow us to see.

The Lord knows that there are some things that we can bear to see.

The Lord knows that there are some things that we can't bear to see.

If the Lord allowed us to see everything going on in this world, we wouldn't be able to bear all the things that we see from day to day.

There are some things that the Lord will allow us to see that will cause you and me to squint our eyes.

There are some things that the Lord will allow you and me to see that will cause us to frown.

There are some things that the Lord will allow you and me to see that will cause us to cry.

There are some things that the Lord will allow you and me to see that will cause us to get angry.

There are some things that the Lord will allow you and me to see that will cause us to walk away.

There are some things that the Lord will allow us to see that will cause us to do something about it.

There are some things that the Lord will allow us to see that will cause us to change our minds.

There are some things that the Lord will allow us to see that will cause us to have nothing to say.

There are some things that the Lord will allow us to see that will cause us to smile.

There are some things that the Lord will allow us to see that will cause us to laugh.

There are some things that the Lord will allow us to see that will cause us to ask some questions.

There are some things that the Lord will allow us to see that will cause us to wonder.

There are some things that the Lord will allow us to see that will cause us to be thankful for Him.

There are some things that the Lord will allow you and me to see that will cause us to be more careful.

There are some things that the Lord will allow you and me to see that will cause us to love trust and obey Him more and more.

A Heavy Blow

Life can give us a heavy blow, especially when we lose loved ones who we were very close to.

Life is giving many people a heavy blow right now.

Many people have lost their jobs and don't have any money to pay their mortgage or rent.

Right now, many people don't have any food to eat and don't have any clean water to drink.

Life can give us a heavy blow when we may least expect it to happen to us.

Life is giving many people a heavy blow right now.

Many people are sick and dying from a bad illness.

Many people right now are very depressed.

Many people have a mental illness that is hard to cope with.

Life can give us a heavy blow, especially if we make a big mistake that might cause other people to suffer or die.

Right now, many people can't sleep at night.

Many people have loss of memory.

Many people are deaf.

Many people are blind and many people can't talk right now.

Life is giving many people a heavy blow right now.

Many people are homeless and many people are giving up on life.

Right now, many people are being discriminated against.

Many people are facing prejudice.

Right now, many people are falsely accused of something that they didn't do.

Life can give us a heavy blow, especially if we turn our backs on Jesus Christ, our Lord.

We will suffer in some kind of way for Jesus' sake, but it also is no comparison to a heavy blow that life can give us.

Life is giving many people a heavy blow right now.

Many people have lost their arms, hands, legs, and feet.

Many children are without mothers and fathers.

Many babies are born blind, deaf, or without arms or legs.

No matter how life can give us a heavy blow, Jesus Christ has given up His life on the cross to save us from our sins.

No matter how life can give us a heavy blow, Jesus rose from the grave to give us eternal life.

In the eternal life there will be no heavy blows to those who are saved in Jesus.

Our Trials Can't Stop

Our trials can't stop the sun from shining on us.

Our trials can't stop the stars from sparkling.

Our trials can't stop the moonlight from glowing.

Our trials can't stop the rain from falling out of the sky.

Our trials can't stop the snow from falling out of the sky.

Our trials can't stop the rivers from flowing.

Our trials can't stop the flowers from blooming.

Our trials can't stop the seasons from changing.

Our trials can't stop the birds from flying.

Our trials can't stop the ocean waves from splashing against the rocks.

Our trials can't stop the dogs from barking.

Our trials can't stop the cats from meowing.

Our trials can't stop the crops from growing.

Our trials can't stop you and me from praying to the Lord.

Our trials can't stop you and me from obeying the Lord.

Our trials can't stop you and me from trusting the Lord.

Our trials can't stop you and me from being saved in the Lord.

Our trials can't stop the wind from blowing.

Our trials can't stop the sky from hovering over us.

Our trials can't stop the grass from growing.

Our trials can't stop the trees from growing tall.

Our trials can't stop the dew from falling.

Our trials can't stop the ground from being under our feet.

Our trials can't stop you and me from loving the Lord Jesus Christ.

Our trials can't stop you and me from loving our neighbors.

Our trials can't stop you and me from putting our hope in the Lord Jesus Christ.

Our trials can't stop you and me from having faith in Jesus Christ, our Lord.

Our trials can't stop our Lord Jesus from cleansing us from our sins.

Our trials can't stop our Lord Jesus Christ from saving us from our sins.

Our trials can't stop our Lord Jesus Christ from bringing us through our trials.

Our trials can't stop our Lord Jesus Christ from giving us the strength to get through our trials.

Our trials can't stop you and me from living our lives unto Jesus Christ.

Our trials can't stop you and me from loving one another.

Our trials can't stop you and me from being witness of Jesus Christ.

Our trials can't stop you and me from winning souls to Jesus Christ.

Our trials can't stop our Lord Jesus Christ from being for us.

It's No Excuse

No matter how bad someone hurt your heart, it is no excuse to not keep your faith in Jesus Christ.

No matter how many bad things you have been through, it's no excuse to not keep your trust in Jesus Christ.

No matter what bad thing you are going through right now, it's no excuse to not hold onto Jesus Christ.

No matter how many enemies you have, it's no excuse to not keep your eyes on Jesus Christ.

No matter how many mistakes you made, it's no excuse to not deny yourself and pick up your cross to follow Jesus Christ.

No matter how many people let you down, it's no excuse to not keep your hope in Jesus Christ.

No matter how many people don't love you, it's no excuse to not love Jesus Christ.

No matter how many people do you wrong, it's no excuse to not obey Jesus Christ.

No matter who turns their back on you, it's no excuse to turn your back on Jesus Christ.

Jesus Christ, our Lord and Savior, loves you and me forever — more than we can ever imagine.

No matter what we have been through and no matter what we are going through, Jesus is for us and not against us.

No matter how many times you have failed, it's no excuse to not give your heart to Jesus, who cannot fail you.

There is no imperfection in Jesus Christ.

When Jesus lived here in this sinful world, He was victorious over every temptation that the devil tried to tempt Him with.

You and I can get the victory in Jesus for putting our trust in Him.

No matter what seems impossible to you and me, it's no excuse to not give our doubts to Jesus Christ.

Jesus can make the impossible possible for you and me.

The Devil's Mind-Control Techniques

The devil causes many people to believe that what they say wrong is right.

The devil causes many people to believe that what they do wrong is right.

The devil causes many people to believe that they have a good reason to kill people.

The devil causes many people to believe that their good works can save them.

The devil causes many people to believe that they are saved through God's grace and don't have to keep God's commandments.

The devil causes many people to believe that after they die they will live again in the form of an animal.

The devil causes many people to believe that they have no sins to confess and repent of.

The devil causes many people to believe that a man can forgive them of their sins.

The devil causes many people to believe that they can talk to their dead loved ones.

The devil causes many people to believe that the Bible is not true.

The devil causes many people to believe that they can live in their sins and make it to heaven.

The devil causes many people to believe that they are better than others.

The devil causes many people to believe that everyone doesn't have human rights.

The devil causes many people to believe that they are worthless.

The devil causes many people to believe that there is no devil.

The devil causes many people to believe that Jesus Christ is not the creator of all things.

The devil causes many people to believe that a lie is the truth and the truth is a lie.

The devil caused the Pharisees to believe that Jesus Christ was the devil.

The devil caused the Pharisees to believe that Jesus Christ was not the Son of God.

The devil caused the Pharisees to believe that Jesus Christ was a blasphemer.

The devil's mind-control techniques are nothing new today.

The devil's mind-control techniques have been around for thousands of years.

The devil causes many people to believe that they are self-made.

The devil causes many people to believe that when they die they will go to heaven before Jesus comes back again.

The devil causes many people to believe that God doesn't love them.

The Devil Has His Human Agents

The devil has his human agents who will tell you and me lies that they want you and me to believe are the truth.

The devil has his human agents who won't give you and me what we deserve.

The devil has his human agents even in the church.

There are people in the church who will deceive you and me and make us believe that they are honest, when they are not honest.

The devil has his human agents who will steal from you and me, and kill you and me with joy in their hearts.

The devil has his human agents who are very selfish and only think about themselves and getting worldly gain.

The devil has his human agents who love to use you and me to help them prosper.

The devil has his human agents who don't care if you and I lose everything that we have.

The devil had his human agents who gave Jesus Christ, our Lord, a hard time when He lived here on earth.

The devil had his human agents who tried to make Jesus look bad.

The devil had his human agents who nailed Jesus on the cross.

The devil has his human agents today that are full of pride, jealousy, and greed.

The devil has his human agents today who will come in the church and cause strife and division amongst church members.

The devil has his human agents who go to church to draw attention to themselves, because they don't want Jesus to get your attention and my attention.

The devil has his human agents who will smile in our faces and plan evil deeds against you and me.

The devil has his human agents who want you and me to believe that they are Christians, when they are living in their sins.

The devil has his human agents who will cause you and me to believe that they are fair with us, when they are cheating us.

Many People Live By

Many people live by the things that they see.

Many people live by their jobs.

Many people live by their education.

Many people live by their skills.

Many people live by their talents.

Many people live by their wealth.

Many people live by their money in the bank.

Many people live by their retirement.

Many people live by their careers.

Many people live by eyesight.

Many people live by their greed for worldly gain.

Many People live by their lust of the flesh.

Many people don't live by faith in Jesus Christ, because they don't believe that Jesus can supply all of their needs — they don't believe that Jesus will never fail them.

Many people will live by their appetite.

Many people will live by the house they live in.

Many People will live by their car.

Many people will live by their truck.

Many people will live by their airplanes.

Many people will live by the clothes on their backs.

Many people will live by the things that they see.

They believe that the things they see can secure their lives.

Many people will live by their hairstyles.

Many people will live by their pets.

Many people will live by the money that they saved up.

Many people will live by their paychecks.

Many people will not live in faith by Jesus Christ, because they don't believe that Jesus can make a way out of no way for them — they don't believe that Jesus can open doors for them.

Many people will live by their jewelry.

Many people will live by their good looks.

Many people will live by their business.

Many people will live by whatever they can get their hands on.

Many people don't believe that Jesus can work anything out for them.

The Lord Can Prepare Us

The Lord can prepare us, even when we don't realize that the Lord can prepare us for what is ahead of us.

We live our lives from day to day, not knowing what could come up next.

The Lord always knows what will come up next, every second, minute, and hour of the day.

We can often be so unaware of what we need to see and what we need to do.

The Lord can prepare us for the unknown that creeps up on us and shocks us.

The Lord always knows how to prepare us to go through our trials.

The Lord always knows how to prepare us to come out victorious over the bad things that can come our way.

The Lord can prepare us years ahead of time to be a blessing to others who may be going through some hardships.

The Lord can prepare us to be strong when storms of difficulties come our way.

We can't always prepare ourselves like the Lord, who can always prepare us on time to face up to our challenges in this life.

We all are different, but the Lord knows how to prepare us in different ways to be a witness for Him.

No one else can prepare you and me better than the Lord and Savior, Jesus Christ.

He knows how to prepare us to get back up when we fall down into thinking sinful thoughts or saying sinful words.

The Lord can also prepare a fool to wise up and do what is right.

You and I don't always know what is ahead of us, and we can't be prepared to fix our problems.

The Lord prepares us to know Him through His holy word.

The Lord prepares us to know one another through His holy word.

The Lord prepares us to know the schemes of the devil.

The Lord can always prepare us to love what is good and shun what is evil.

I Wrestled with the Lord

I wrestled with the Lord all night long in my mind.

I had a lot of things on my mind that I needed to talk to the Lord about.

I talked to the Lord about my family.

I talk to the Lord about my kinfolks.

I talked to the Lord about my church family.

I talked to the Lord about my next-door neighbors.

I talked to the Lord about this nation's leaders.

I talked to the Lord about my friends.

I talked to the Lord about myself.

I had a real good talk with the Lord, all night long.

My good Lord Jesus Christ listened to what I had to say to Him.

The more I talked to the Lord, the more I didn't want to stop talking.

I wrestled with the Lord all night long in my mind, until He blessed me.

My Lord Jesus Christ blessed me in my mind.

He gave me peace of mind.

He answered my prayers in the early morning sunlight.

I didn't let the Lord go in my mind until I knew I felt much better in the early morning sunlight, then I finally got some sleep.

I wrestled with the Lord all night long in my mind that was heavy with the things that I have no control over.

I wrestled with the Lord all night long in my mind that was heavy with the uncertainty of life.

The Lord blessed my mind and took away the heavy burdens in my mind.

I am so glad that I chose to not let Jesus go as I wrestled with Jesus all night long.

Jesus strengthened my mind and cleansed my mind from filthy things of the world.

I felt so brand new in my mind because I didn't let my Lord Jesus go as I wrestled with Him all night long and He blessed me.

Love Is Not

Love is not a light switch that can be turned on or off.

Love is a light that stays on all the time.

There are people who turn love on and off like a light switch.

They turn their love on when they want something from you.

They turn their love off if you don't give them what they want.

Love is not part-time.

There are people who will take some time off from loving you.

They will avoid your phone calls until they need something from you.

Love is full-time like working a full-time job.

Love can sometimes be like working a hard job.

There are people who are hard to love — you and I have to work hard at loving them.

Love is not a split personality that changes on us.

Love will never change on us.

We can trust love.

We can't trust a split personality.

Love is not cautious of us.

A dog will bark at you and me because of being cautious of us.

There are people who are like a dog barking at you and me who haven't done anything wrong to them — they will make up things that we haven't done to them.

Love won't bark at you and me.

Love will wag its tail at us for us to rub its head and back.

Love is not a rug that we can walk all over.

There are people who will walk all over your love and my love for them.

They believe that they have a right to do that.

Love will not keep its distance from us.

There are people who will keep their distance from us.

We haven't done anything wrong to them yet they assume that we are not worth getting close to.

Love is not criticizing.

There are people who will criticize us if we don't have any passion for doing the things that they are passionate about doing.

Love is not favoritism.

There are people who have their favorite ones who they love to talk to.

God shows no favoritism.

God loves everyone the same.

We are all wonderfully made by God.

God is worthy to be God, who is love through His Son, Jesus Christ.

We can't truly understand or imagine how deep God's love for us is.

Jesus Christ, Our Lord, Is the Living Truth

Jesus Christ, our Lord, is the living truth.

Jesus is the living truth above the truth that we speak.

Jesus is the living truth above the truth that we live.

Jesus Christ, our Lord, is the living truth.

Jesus is the living truth that we see.

Jesus is the living truth above the truth that we hear.

Jesus Christ, our Lord, is the living truth.

Jesus is the living truth above the truth that can set us free.

Jesus is the living truth above the truth that we believe.

Jesus Christ, our Lord, is the living truth.

There is no lie in Jesus Christ.

There are many brilliant liars in this world.

There are many professional liars in this world.

There are many intelligent liars in this world.

There are many stupid liars in this world.

Jesus Christ, our Lord, is the living truth.

Jesus is the living truth above the truth that many people won't tell.

Jesus is the living truth above the truth that many people won't believe.

Jesus Christ, our Lord, is the living truth.

Jesus is the living truth above the truth that many people won't accept.

Jesus is the living truth above the truth that many people will deny.

Jesus Christ our Lord is the living truth.

There are many crazy liars in this world.

There are many good liars in this world.

There are many bad liars in this world.

Jesus Christ, our Lord, is the living truth.

There are many sick liars in this world.

There are many violent liars in this world.

There are many proud liars in this world.

Jesus Christ, our Lord, is the living truth.

Jesus cannot lie to us.

Jesus Christ, our Lord, is the living truth.

Jesus cannot lie to any race, creed, or culture of people.

Jesus cannot lie to any nation of people.

Jesus Christ, our Lord, is the only living truth to set you and me free from lying to ourselves the most.

Owe Them Something

There are people who you don't know who will act like you owe them something.

They will act like that you owe them something if you don't say anything to them.

There are people who will act like you owe them something if you don't look at them.

There are people who have a lot of messed up ways because of being so judgmental of others.

It doesn't matter what age people are.

A lot of people have many selfish ways.

We all owe our lives to the Lord.

We all owe everything that we have to the Lord.

There are people who will give you the evil look if they feel like you owe them something.

There are people who will talk badly about you if they feel like you owe them something.

There are people who won't like you if they feel like you owe them something.

There are people who you know and some of them may feel like you owe them something.

Some people in the church may feel like you owe them something if you don't click with them.

We owe it all to Jesus Christ who has every right to claim everything that we owe Him.

We owe Jesus our full attention every day.

We owe Jesus our thoughts.

We owe Jesus our words.

We owe Jesus our actions.

We owe Jesus our bodies.

We owe Jesus our minds.

We owe Jesus our hearts every day.

Only Jesus always deserves what we owe Him.

We owe Jesus our accomplishments.

We owe Jesus our successes.

We owe Jesus our victories.

We owe Jesus our faith.

We owe Jesus our sacrifices.

We owe Jesus our existence.

We owe Jesus our destiny.

Jesus Christ, our Lord and Savior, can always handle whatever we owe Him.

Jesus Christ will always be fair about everything that we owe Him.

Jesus will never add on more than what we owe Him.

Problems

From the smallest problems to the biggest problems, the Lord is always concerned to solve every problem.

The Lord will not overlook the smallest problems that you and I can overlook.

A little rooftop water leak can become a big rooftop water leak if it is not repaired, this shows that a small problem can become a big problem if it is left unattended.

We tend to take the small problems lightly, as if they are no big deal to not take care of.

The Lord will never take our small problems lightly.

The Lord knows that our small problems can become big problems if we let them go unchecked day after day.

We very often want to take care of our big problems and won't want to waste any time to attend to the small ones.

We can easily not want to take care of our small problems, and can put them off like they don't exist.

A little cancer can spread all through the body if we don't get treatment for it in its early stages.

A small problem can become a big problem if it is left alone.

Not only a big problem but a small problem will not go unattended to the Lord.

The Lord shows no favoritism to our big problems — they are of no bigger concern to the Lord than our small problems are.

The Lord is equally concerned about all of our problems.

You and I can be more concerned about our big problems than our small problems.

We can overlook the small problems in our home, where they can become big problems.

We can overlook the small problems in the church, where they can become a problems.

A small pot on the stove left unchecked can burn down a big house.

A small infection can become a big infection if it is left untreated.

Not only big problems but also small problems are important to the Lord.

The Pathway

Treating people right is the pathway of life that Jesus gives to us — we should live to be good to everybody.

Having good motives and good intentions is the pathway of life that Jesus gives to us to live with a pure heart.

Not judging people is the pathway of life that Jesus gives to us to live and not assume anything about anyone we don't know.

Being fair to everyone is the pathway of life that Jesus gives to us to live so we give people equal opportunity day after day.

Showing respect to everybody is the pathway of life that Jesus gives to us to live so we don't believe that we are better than others.

Helping people if we can help them is the pathway of life that Jesus gives us to live so we are not selfish.

Loving people for who they are is the pathway of life that Jesus gives to us to live so we get along with people who may be different from us.

Praying for people is the pathway of life that Jesus gives to us to live and believe that Jesus can change people who want to change for the better.

Living right by example is the pathway of life that Jesus gives to us to live a holy and righteous life before people who are living in the darkness of their sins.

Loving and obeying Jesus Christ, our Lord, is the pathway of life that Jesus gives us to live in.

Using our spiritual gifts is the pathway of life that Jesus gives to us to live so we can build up His church with people who confess and repent of their sins unto Jesus Christ and then get baptized to live for Jesus.

Choices

We are not always aware of making all the right choices.

We can make the wrong choice, because it could be camouflaged to look like the right choice to make.

We are not perfect and don't make all the right choices all the time.

We can believe that we are making the right choice about something, when it may be the wrong choice.

We must pray and ask the Lord to help us make the right choices, because we can't make all the right choices just using our own intellect.

We can't make all the right choices using our own strength.

We can't make all the right choices using our own will.

We need the Lord to help us to make all the right choices.

God's holy word is truth to encourage us to make the right choices.

God's holy word gives us knowledge to make the right choices.

We can make the wrong choice out of ignorance.

We can make the wrong choice out of anger.

We can make the wrong choice out of pride.

We can make the wrong choice because we are being hasty.

We can make the wrong choice when we aren't paying attention.

We can make the wrong choice out of greed.

We can make the wrong choice out of jealousy.

We can make the wrong choice out of selfishness.

We can make the wrong choice and not realize it.

We can make the wrong choice and may never see it.

If we made all the right choices all the time, then we would be perfect.

We have a sinful nature and we will make the wrong choice sooner or later in life.

If we make all the right choices all the time, then we would never have to confess or repent.

Making choices is a lifetime thing.

We make choices twenty-four hours a day, around the clock.

The best right choice that anyone can make is to choose to believe in Jesus Christ, who can save us from our sins.

Regardless of our sinful nature, we can still choose Jesus.

Knowledge

Many people will use their knowledge for good deeds.

Many people will use their knowledge to do evil things.

Many people will use their Bible knowledge to try to be Lord over the church flock.

Many people will use their education knowledge to try to control people.

Many people will use their education knowledge to use people.

Many people will use their education knowledge to deceive people.

Knowledge is powerful and can save many people's lives.

Knowledge is powerful and can cause many people to get rich.

Knowledge is powerful and can prolong many people's lives.

Knowledge is powerful and can cause many people to prosper in life.

A fool will use knowledge to cheat people out of their money.

A fool will use knowledge for selfish reasons.

A fool will use knowledge to steal from people.

A fool will use knowledge to do foolish things.

Good people will use knowledge to help people.

Good people will use knowledge to encourage people.

Good people will use knowledge to unite people.

Good people will use knowledge to teach other people good things.

Bible knowledge is the most powerful knowledge that you can ever get.

Bible knowledge lets us know who God is.

Bible knowledge lets us know who the devil is.

Bible knowledge lets us know who we are.

Bible knowledge lets us know the right way to live.

Bible knowledge lets us know who Jesus Christ is.

Bible knowledge lets us know what could be our destiny.

Bible knowledge lets us know where we came from.

Bible knowledge lets us know that we are sinners who Jesus can save from being lost.

Bible knowledge lets us know that God is love.

Within You

If you have peace within you, don't let any troublemakers take away your inner peace.

If you have kindness within you, don't let no mean person take away your kindness.

If you have joy within you, don't let unhappy people take away your joy.

If you have control within you, don't let any out of control person take away your control.

If you have trust within you, don't let untrustworthy people take away your trust.

If you have fairness within you, do not let an unfair person take away your fairness.

If you have a truth within you, don't let a liar take away your truth.

If you have good reasoning within you, don't let an unreasonable person take away your good reason.

If you have positive thoughts within you, don't let a negative person take away your positivity.

If you have love within you, don't let a hate filled person take away your love.

If you have good opinions within you, don't let a person with bad opinions take away your good ones.

If you feel good within you, don't let a depressed person take away your good feelings.

If you know what is right within you, don't let a doubtful person take away your righteous feelings.

If you have faith in Jesus Christ within you, don't let an unbeliever take away your faith in Jesus Christ.

If you have works from the Lord within you, don't let someone who is not working for the Lord take away your works from the Lord.

If you have Jesus within you, don't let anyone take away Jesus from within you.

Can't Put Our Trust in Tomorrow

You and I can't put our trust in a tomorrow that we may not live to see.

Many people will put their trust in tomorrow, but they might not live to see it.

You and I can say what we will do tomorrow, but we have no clue if we might die today.

It's not good to say, "I will do this tomorrow" and "I will do that tomorrow" because today will laugh at us — it is the Lord's will what we will and won't do and whether we will live to see tomorrow.

Only fools will not acknowledge the Lord's will that they will live to see tomorrow.

Tomorrow is no sure thing that we will see.

All of today is no sure thing that we will live to see.

Being alive today is a miracle from the Lord.

If you and I live to see tomorrow, it will be a miracle from the Lord.

Tomorrow is like a question and only the Lord can always answer it.

You and I can't put our trust in tomorrow, even if we believe we will see it.

Many people believe that they will live to see tomorrow, but they didn't know that they would die today.

You and I can only put our trust in the Lord Jesus Christ, who tomorrow will bow down unto and obey.

All of our yesterdays obeyed Jesus for us to see today.

All of today will obey Jesus, if He commands today to be for us to live.

Tomorrow is like a mountain that no one can climb if the Lord causes it to tremble.

You and I can't put our trust in tomorrow, because it can be broken like pieces of glass that can cut our hands if we pick it up.

You and I cannot put our trust in tomorrow, because it can be like running very fast down the stairs with our eyes closed — we will surely fall and hurt ourselves.

You and I can't put our trust in tomorrow, because it is like a big spider crawling on us and biting us in our sleep.

You and I can put all of our trust in our Lord and Savior Jesus Christ, who tomorrow will come to with no hidden agendas.

Love to Use People

The people the devil loves to use the most are genius people.

The people the devil loves to use the most are brilliant people.

The people the devil loves to use the most are intelligent people.

The people the devil loves to use the most are smart people.

The people the devil loves to use the most are educated people.

The devil knows that the smarter you are, the more influence you can have on people who are not as smart as you.

The people the devil loves to use the most are very clever people.

The people the devil loves to use the most are very charming people.

The people the devil loves to use the most are very attractive people.

The devil knows that the more beautiful you are, the more influence you can have on people.

The devil is all about showing favoritism to people who can benefit him the most.

The Lord shows no favoritism to anyone — He loves to use everyone.

The Lord loves to use everyone, no matter if they're educated or not so educated.

The Lord loves to use everyone, no matter if they're a genius or not a genius.

The Lord loves to use everyone, no matter if they're brilliant or not brilliant.

The Lord loves to use everyone, no matter if they're intelligent or not so intelligent.

The Lord loves to use everyone, no matter if they're smart or not so smart.

The Lord loves to use everyone, no matter if they're very attractive or not very attractive.

The Lord loves to use everyone, no matter if they're beautiful or not so beautiful.

The Lord loves to use everyone, no matter if they're rich or poor.

The Lord loves to use everyone, no matter if they're great or not so great.

The Lord shows no favoritism.

He doesn't love me more than He loves you, and He doesn't love you more than He loves me.

The Lord can make an uneducated person brilliant in some kind of way.

The Lord loves to use everyone who He shed His blood on the cross and died on the cross to save from being lost in sin that has an influence on everyone every day.

Stories

Stories are proof of people who lived thousands of years before us.

Stories are proof of people who lived hundreds of years before us.

Stories are proof of people who lived decades of years before us.

Stories let us know that there were people who did some good things.

Stories let us know that there were people who did some bad things.

Stories let us know where we come from.

Stories let us know where we are headed to.

Stories let us know there is no new thing under the sun.

Stories let us know that we can do the same things today that people did many years ago.

Stories can give us good advice.

Stories can teach us something good to hold onto.

Stories can help us to wise up.

Stories can change our lives for the better.

The older the stories are, the more they can amaze us.

The Bible's stories are the best stories that can ever be told to us.

Many people don't believe the stories in the Bible.

Many people today believe that the Bible stories are fairy tale stories.

All of the stories in the Bible let us know what kind of world we live in.

The stories in the Bible can sure give us a true awakening for our lives.

The Bible stories are the telescope of life for us to see the past, present, and future.

The Bible stories are the microscope that can show us how to create our own destiny.

God is Fair

God is fair to punish whoever disobeys Him.

God is fair to judge everyone who can choose to do good or evil.

God is fair to let us reap what we sow.

God is fair to let us say what we want to say.

God is fair to let us do what we want to do.

God is fair to let anyone come to Him and repent.

God is fair to let anyone stray away from Him.

God is fair to give us our reward in heaven one day.

God is fair to give us another chance.

God is fair to let anyone be overly wicked.

God is fair to let anyone be overly righteous.

God is fair to destroy the wicked one day.

God is fair to let the devil tempt us.

God is fair to accept the choices that we make.

God is fair to warn us to not say something wrong.

God is fair to not answer all of our prayers.

God is fair with His reasons to not answer all of our prayers.

God is fair to let anyone make a fool out of himself or herself.

God is fair to shorten anyone's life.

God is all-knowing to know if it is best to shorten your life or my life.

God is fair to let anyone live a long life — God knows if that's what it will take to save a soul from being lost.

God is fair to let anyone go through some hardships — God knows if it will be humble you and me.

God is fair to let anyone question Him, even though His answer may not be what anyone may want to accept.

God was fair to give us His only begotten Son to save us from our sins.

God is fair to let His Son come back again to take all of His righteous children to heaven one day.

To Make it to Heaven

I want to make it to heaven.

I want all of my loved ones to make it to heaven.

I want all of my kinfolks to make it to heaven.

I want all of my neighbors to make it to heaven.

I want all of my brothers and sisters in the church to make it to heaven.

Regardless of what I want, everybody won't make it to heaven.

Everybody will not believe in Jesus Christ and be saved.

Everybody will not love Jesus.

Everybody will not obey Jesus.

So many people will be lost in their sins.

So many people are lost in their sins.

So many people don't care about being saved in Jesus.

Jesus Christ gave up His life on the cross and rose from the grave for everybody to be saved in Him who will take us to heaven to live with Him forever and ever.

This old world will pass away one day.

Nothing in this world will be left behind to hold onto.

Heaven is eternal for immortal people to live in.

The only immortal people will be born again believers in Jesus Christ, who is coming back again one day to take you and me to heaven for being saved in Him.

As bad as people can be, we Christians want them to wise up and confess and repent of their sins unto the Lord.

We Christians want bad people to give their lives to the Lord before it's too late.

We Christians want to make it to heaven and we don't want anyone to be lost.

We don't want anyone to miss out on heaven.

God gives everybody free will choices.

Everybody will not make Jesus Christ their choice and love Him and obey Him.

Jesus is our only hope to make it to heaven.

Jesus is our only way to make it to heaven.

No human being has a heaven to put us in.

If a human being had a heaven to put us in, then he or she might very well pick and choose who to put in their heaven.

Jesus doesn't pick and choose who He wants to put in His heaven.

It doesn't matter to Jesus if you are rich or poor.

It doesn't matter to Jesus if you are educated or uneducated.

Jesus does have limits because He will not put any wicked person in His heaven.

Jesus will only put the righteous people in His heaven.

Heaven is a place for all who love and obey Jesus Christ.

Sinful people cannot enter into heaven.

Jesus had to cast Lucifer out of heaven because he refused to confess and repent of his sins, just like his fallen angels.

We Should Not Let Temporary Things

We should not let temporary things cause us to be lost in our sins.

We should not let anything in this temporary world cause us to lose our souls.

We should love Jesus Christ first and above everyone else and everything else in this world.

In this temporary world we are only temporary and will one day die.

We should love to live our lives unto Jesus, who is coming back again one day soon.

We should want to be saved in Jesus, who is the only one who will give you and me an immortal body.

Jesus will give us a new, perfect body when He comes back again.

Jesus will give us a perfect mind.

Jesus will give us a perfect heart.

Jesus will give us a perfect life that we will live forever and ever.

Jesus will put us in a perfect place to live — that perfect place is heaven.

If we love and obey Jesus in this temporary world, He will save us and take us to live with Him in a perfect world one day.

The new world that Jesus will create will be eternal.

Jesus will make you and me eternal one day, when He comes back again.

We should not let temporary things cause us to turn our backs on Jesus Christ.

Jesus Christ is eternal life that we should always look forward to receiving one day.

This temporary world will one day pass away.

We will live forever and ever with Jesus, if we are saved in Him.

Life goes on and on in Jesus after death.

Jesus will come back again and raise all the righteous dead to live forever and ever with Him one day.

We should not let temporary things be our God.

We should not worship temporary things.

We should not put temporary things above the Lord Jesus Christ.

Don't Be Ashamed

Don't be ashamed of the gospel of Jesus Christ.

Don't be ashamed to give a testimony about Jesus.

Don't be ashamed to be a witness of Jesus.

Don't be ashamed to live unto Jesus.

The Pharisees tried to put Jesus Christ to shame.

The Pharisees called Jesus a blasphemer for admitting that He was the Son of God.

The mob tried to shame Jesus by wanting to crucify Him.

The Roman soldiers tried to shame Jesus by nailing Him on the cross.

Back in the Bible days, to be hung on a cross was reserved for the worst kind of criminals.

Those criminals were put to shame by being hung on a cross.

Many people looked at Jesus with shame when He was hung on the cross.

Those people didn't believe in Jesus Christ.

Jesus was perfect, without sin and was no criminal.

Jesus didn't deserve to die on a cross.

In the eyes of law keepers, the cross represented shame.

Many people looked down on Jesus when He was nailed to the cross.

They didn't realize that Jesus was not ashamed to die on the cross for all of their sins.

The Pharisees and mob and Roman soldiers didn't realize that Jesus was not ashamed to die on the cross in their place.

If Jesus Christ was ashamed of sinners like you and me, then He would have never come to this sinful world.

If Jesus Christ was ashamed of sinners, then He would have never lived in this world among sinners.

If Jesus Christ was ashamed of sinners like you and me, then Jesus would have never given up His life on the cross that represents the shame of criminals.

Don't be ashamed to talk about Jesus when the opportunity comes around.

Don't be ashamed to work for Jesus with the spiritual gifts that He gives to all those who are saved in Him.

Don't be ashamed to spread the gospel of Jesus Christ.

Jesus is not ashamed to save us from our sins and give us His free gift of eternal life.

Fault

There are people who will find fault in what you say.

There are people who find fault in what you do.

There are people who will find fault in what you don't do.

There are people who will find faults in you and me.

There are people who won't admit their own faults.

There are people who love to talk about your faults.

There are people who will see your faults and my faults.

There are people who won't see their own faults.

There are people who don't want to see their own faults.

There are people who love to point out your faults and my faults.

There are people who believe that they have no faults.

There are people who believe that they can do nothing wrong.

There are people who believe that they can say nothing wrong.

The Pharisees tried to find fault in Jesus Christ, who they told lies to and tried to make themselves look good.

There are people who will never admit their faults.

There are people who are very good at finding faults in you and me.

There are people who believe that they are so right about finding faults in you and me.

There are people who will find fault in the Lord God, if God doesn't answer their prayers.

There are people who will find fault in Jesus Christ, our Lord and our God, for letting their loved ones die.

It is so easy to find fault in someone else, and it's hard for a selfish person to see their own faults.

Only Jesus had no faults when He lived Here on earth without sin.

Everybody in this world has some faults, and nobody should point a finger at other people's faults.

We will all fall short of the glory of God.

Faultfinding people will reap what they sow.

Faultfinding people believe they are perfect in their own eyes.

Faultfinding is like seeing your own shadow and pretending like it's not there and doesn't do as you do.

The Lord Will Test Our Love

The Lord will test our love for one another when we just don't know and don't see the Lord's test.

The Lord always knows if we will pass His test of our love.

The Lord always knows if you and I love some of our brothers and sisters more than others.

The Lord hates it if we show disrespect to people, especially in the church where there is no big me and little you and no big you and little me.

The Lord will test our love for one another when we pretend like we all have our lives together and want the Lord to agree with everything that we say and do.

Sermons can be preached about the Lord, we can sing songs about the Lord, and we can give daily devotions about the Lord but if you and I don't truly love one another, we will fail the Lord's test of love.

We all love being blessed by the Lord and can truly thank Him for His many blessings that He gives to us every day.

We can truly thank the Lord for His grace and mercy that He gives to us, but we can't overlook how much we need to love one another every day.

We Christians pretty much know not to overlook God's blessings upon our lives.

We pretty much know not to overlook God's mercy and grace upon our lives, but when it comes to truly loving one another we can get absent-minded and overlook God's love for everybody in the church and outside the church.

You and I will fall short of truly loving everybody in the church and outside of the church.

We all need Jesus Christ, our Lord, to help us to truly love one another and, most of all, to love Him every day — that is the Lord's test of our love.

We all can give a good talk but we must also walk the walk, especially when it comes to loving the Lord and loving one another because those things go together every day.

The Unknown

I don't have to fear the unknown.

I can put my trust in the Lord, who knows all things in heaven and on earth and beneath the earth.

The Lord knows all of my past, the Lord knows all of my present, and the Lord knows all of my future.

I don't have to fear what I don't know.

The Lord can protect me from the unknown.

The Lord is forever more powerful than the unknown.

I don't remember all of my past, I don't know all of my present, and I don't know my future — it is unknown to me.

There is nothing that the Lord doesn't know.

What I don't know, the Lord can make known to me.

If I keep my faith, the Lord won't let the unknown burden me or bring me down.

The unknown is in the hands of the Lord.

The Lord can crush the unknown and keep it from crushing my hope in Him.

The unknown will try to discourage me.

I can keep my trust in the Lord to put the unknown under my feet.

The unknown will try to make me weak.

My strength is from the Lord, who keeps me going strong in Him.

The unknown will try to depress me.

The Lord will prepare me to get the victory over the unknown, if I obey His voice telling me what I need to do.

The unknown has no authority over my life, if I live my life fully surrendered unto the Lord day after day.

The unknown can't do to me more than what the Lord allows it to do.

The Lord won't leave me helpless to the unknown if I love Him with all of my mind, heart, soul, and strength.

The unknown will try to make me unaware of the things that could go wrong in my life.

The Lord will give me His Holy Spirit to make me aware of things that I need to know, if I am willing to take heed and obey His still quiet voice.

Do Not Weigh More

My bad days do not weigh more than my blessings from the Lord.

My disappointments do not weigh more than my blessings from the Lord.

My grief does not weigh more than my blessings from the Lord.

It's a blessing from the Lord to have eyes to see.

It's a blessing from the Lord to have ears to hear.

It is a blessing from the Lord to have hands.

It's a blessing from the Lord to have arms.

It's a blessing from the Lord to have legs.

It's a blessing from the Lord to have feet.

It's a blessing from the Lord to have good mental health.

It's a blessing from the Lord to be in good physical health.

My trials do not weigh more than my blessings from the Lord.

My blessings from the Lord will always weigh more than my misfortunes.

When I die, it's a blessing from the Lord who saves me from my sins for me to even die being saved in Him.

My death won't be worthless because of Jesus Christ coming back again one day to give me eternal life.

Death cannot weigh more than my blessings from the Lord, who died for my sins and rose from the grave with the victory over death for me to live again after I die.

After I die, I will live again in the eternal life that Jesus will give to me when He comes back again on the clouds of glory.

My sins do not weigh more than my blessings from the Lord.

When I was living in my unconfessed and unrepentant sins, the Lord had still given me some of His blessings even though I know I didn't deserve them.

The Lord would have blessed me a lot more if I had been living my life unto Him.

Today I am living my life unto the Lord, who gives me even more blessings to weigh more than any kind of trial I go through.

Whatever problem that comes my way will not weigh more than my blessings from the Lord, who is the president and CEO of the blessings business.

You are Alive

I am so glad my Lord Jesus Christ that You are alive and have all the power, even though many people don't believe in you.

I am so glad, my Lord Jesus, that You are alive and sitting on the right hand side of God's holy throne.

Many people don't believe in You, and You give them that free will choice.

I am so glad, my Lord Jesus Christ, that you are alive forever and ever more beyond this life here on earth that is short.

Many people don't believe in You, who can add more years to anyone's life.

I am so glad, my Lord Jesus, that You are alive and You allow many unbelievers to live over three score and ten years.

I am so glad, my Lord Jesus, that You are alive, regardless of many people who don't believe in You.

They can't stop you from blessing my soul and saving my soul because they don't believe in You.

I am so glad, my Lord Jesus, that you are alive and helping me to keep my faith in You.

Many people have turned their backs on You and believe that it's the right thing to do.

I am so glad, my Lord Jesus Christ, that You are alive and the head of the church.

I am so glad, my Lord Jesus, that you are alive and in charge of everything.

Many people don't believe in You and they believe that they are in charge of their lives.

I am so glad, my Lord Jesus Christ, that you are alive and keeping me strong in You.

Many people don't believe in You and think that they are so strong and right for not believing in You.

They are truly spiritually weak and will die in their sins because of not believing in You, my holy Lord Jesus Christ.

I am so glad, my Lord Jesus Christ, that you are alive up in heaven.

Many people don't believe in You and that You are coming back again one day.

Those people who don't believe in You will one day know in hell that they were so wrong about You.

I Love My Church Family

My church family is not made up of perfect people, but I love my church family.

I love to be in church with my church family.

I love to worship the Lord with my church family.

I love to pray with my church family.

I love to have Bible studies with my church family.

I love to fellowship with my church family.

I love talking to my church family.

The Lord has blessed me with a good church family.

The Lord has brought me a long way with my church family.

My church family is a blessing from the Lord.

My brothers and sisters in the Lord are not perfect people, but I am glad that they are in my life.

My church family helps me to hold onto my Lord Jesus Christ.

My church family helps me to love and obey the Lord.

I want to make it to heaven with my church family.

I love my church family, regardless of them falling short of the glory of God.

My church family and I have come a long way in the Lord.

I love being on one accord with my church family.

I love praying for my church family.

It's an honor and a privilege to go through some trials with my church family.

I want to always be in my church family's lives.

I don't want to ever turn my back on my church family.

I know that my church family is a gift to me from the Lord.

My brothers and sisters in the Lord help me to keep my eyes on the Lord Jesus Christ.

My church family helps me to keep myself humble unto the Lord.

I love growing stronger in the Lord with my church family.

I love holding onto my church family.

My church family is not made up of perfect people, but they are trying their best to love and obey the Lord.

My church family is not made up of perfect people, but they are trying their best to love me even though they can see I am far from being perfect.

My church family helps me to make Jesus my choice every day.

My church family is a small family, but they are strong in the Lord.

My church family knows that this world is not their home.

They know that they are pilgrims passing through this old sinful world.

My church family encourages me and reminds me that I am a pilgrim like them, just passing through this world to get to our destination in heaven one day.

Going Through Trials

Going through trials for Jesus' name sake will draw us closer and closer to Him.

Going through trials for Jesus' name sake will give us strength in the Lord.

Going through trials for Jesus' name sake will encourage us to keep our trust in the Lord.

Going through trials for Jesus' name sake will let us know that this world is not our home.

Going through trials for Jesus' name sake will help us to hold onto the Lord.

Going through trials for Jesus' name sake will let us know that Jesus will never fail us.

Going through trials for Jesus' name sake will let us know that Jesus will bring us through our trials.

Going through trials for Jesus' name sake will encourage us to keep our faith in Him.

Going through trials for Jesus' name sake will encourage us to keep our hope in Him.

Going through trials for Jesus' name sake will give us joy for knowing that we are saved in Jesus.

Going through trials for Jesus' name sake will give us a peace of mind for knowing that Jesus will never leave us or forsake us.

Going through trials for Jesus' name sake will encourage us to not give up on Jesus who will give us the victory over our hardships.

Going through trials for Jesus' name sake will encourage us to keep on striving to live for Jesus until we one day die.

Going through trials for Jesus' name sake will motivate us to never turn our backs on Jesus.

Going through trials for Jesus' name sake will strengthen our relationship with Jesus.

Going through trials for Jesus' name sake will let us know that Jesus is for us and not against us.

Going through trials for Jesus' name sake will let us know that unbelievers will have it much worse on judgment day.

Going through trials for Jesus' name sake will let us know that it is nothing strange to go for His name sake.

Going through trials for Jesus' name sake will let us know that we are going through nothing much at all compared to what Jesus went through to save us from our sins.

We Worship a Holy God

We worship a holy God, because God is holy.

Wearing short and tight dresses to church will take away the holiness out of the divine service.

Wearing flashy and tight suits will take away the holiness of the divine service in the church.

Wearing attractive colors and a lot of makeup will draw attention to yourself in the church.

Jesus Christ our Lord is holy every day.

We Christians are supposed to dress holy in the church and outside the church.

Our worship is worthless to the Lord if we don't dress right before the Lord.

We can have plenty of Bible knowledge.

We can give testimonies about the Lord.

We can tell others about the Lord.

We can love our neighbors

But, if we are misrepresenting Jesus by the way that we dress, how can we be a holy people?

How can we be so different from the people of the world if we dress like them?

If we are wearing our clothes tight, how can we be holy?

We can wear loose clothes that we can buy from the clothing stores.

If we are wearing jewelry, it will take away our holiness.

The people of the world see nothing wrong with wearing short dresses, tight blouses, tight pants, and tight shirts.

The people of the world see nothing wrong about wearing jewelry or fancy hairstyles or having tattoos.

We Christians are supposed to be holy.

We are supposed to put away those worldly things.

We are supposed to worship a holy God.

Many pastors won't preach about how we should dress because they are afraid to step on peoples toes in the church.

If we want to follow Jesus Christ, we must deny ourselves the things that keep us from being like Jesus.

The Lord says that if you know what is right and don't do it, then you have sinned against Him.

If we know that it's wrong to dress inappropriately before the Lord and we still do it, then we are not a holy people before the Lord, no matter what spiritual gifts we have in the church.

Not Waiting on the Lord

Not waiting on the Lord can be a regret for years.

If we don't wait on the Lord, it will catch up with us sooner or later.

We must wait on the Lord to work things out for us.

Waiting on the Lord is always the right thing to do.

Waiting on the Lord will give you and me peace of mind.

Not waiting on the Lord can surely cause us to fail.

Not waiting on the Lord can trouble our minds.

Not waiting on the Lord can wreck our lives.

Not waiting on the Lord can lead us down the road to destruction.

Not waiting on the Lord is a terrible choice to make.

Not waiting on the Lord can cause us to be miserable.

Not waiting on the Lord is a terrible thing to do.

Not waiting on the Lord can shorten our lives.

Not waiting on the Lord can lead us to ruins.

Not waiting on the Lord will sooner or later show and tell our lives.

Not waiting on the Lord can be a terrible experience.

If we wait on the Lord, we will never regret it.

It's always good to wait on the Lord to work out our problems.

It's always good to wait on the Lord to make things better in our lives.

It's always good to wait on the Lord to supply all of our needs.

It's always good to wait on the Lord to answer our prayers.

It's always good to wait on the Lord to show us what we need to do.

Not waiting on the Lord can lead us to tragedy.

Not waiting on the Lord is a foolish thing to do.

Not waiting on the Lord can lead us to hell.

Our time is not always right on time for us and we can fail in what we do and say.

If we wait on the Lord, He will always be there for us right on time.

More and More

The Christian journey will never end.

We need to walk more and more with the Lord.

We need to pray more and more to the Lord.

We need to have more and more faith in the Lord.

We need to trust the Lord more and more.

We need to obey the Lord more and more.

The Christian journey will never end.

It will go on and on in this world and in the new heaven and earth one day soon.

We need to love the Lord more and more.

We need to love one another more and more.

We need to get to know the Lord more and more.

This Christian journey is eternal.

We need to be more and more thankful unto the Lord.

We need to praise the Lord more and more.

We need to reverence the Lord more and more.

We need to be more and more humble unto the Lord.

This Christian journey will go on more when Jesus comes back again to take us to heaven.

The Lord has brought you and me a long way on this journey and we still have a long way to go on this journey that will never end.

Jesus Christ, our Lord and Savior, is everlasting from everlasting for you and me and we need to worship Him more and more.

When Jesus comes back again, He will make you and me immortal and we will need to be more and more like Him in the new heaven and in the new earth that Jesus will create one day.

This Christian journey is nonstop.

We need to do more and more work for the Lord with the spiritual gifts that He gives to us to build up His church.

If you and I only have one spiritual gift from the Lord, we need to use it more and more to win souls to the Lord.

There is no end to Jesus Christ, our Lord, who wants to save more and more people from their sins before He removes His saving grace from this world.

Are Only a Dream

We can thank the Lord that a lot of things are only a dream in our sleep.

We can thank the Lord that a lot of our bad dreams don't come true in the real world.

A lot of our good dreams don't come true.

We can thank the Lord that a lot of our dreams fade away when we wake up from our sleep.

We can have a good dream that seems so real until we wake up and know that it was only a dream.

We can have a bad dream that seems so real until we wake up and know that it was only a dream.

We don't always understand where a dream comes from.

We don't always understand why we dream what we dream.

All we know is that we had a good dream or a bad dream in our sleep.

The Lord always knows where a dream comes from.

The Lord always knows why we dream what we dream in our sleep.

Our dreams that the Lord allows to come true for us are for His reasons and will have favor with us or not have a favor with us.

We have no control over our dreams in our sleep.

Only the Lord has control over our dreams in our sleep.

Our bad dreams can't come true if the Lord doesn't allow them to come true.

We can always thank the Lord Jesus Christ that a lot of our dreams are only dreams that will fade away when we wake up.

The few dreams that do come true the Lord knows that it's for the best to let us know that He is in control of dreams and reality.

We Shouldn't Love to Point Our Fingers

We shouldn't love to point our finger at people's mistakes with God's holy word.

We shouldn't love to point our finger at people's flaws with God's holy word.

We shouldn't love to point our fingers at people's bad choices with God's holy word.

We shouldn't love to point our finger at people's bad deeds with God's holy word.

God's holy word is for us all who have sins that only Jesus Christ, our Lord, can save us from.

We shouldn't love to point our finger at people's mistakes with God's holy word.

We shouldn't have any pleasure in trying to make anyone feel useless, especially for working for the Lord.

We shouldn't love to point our finger at our brothers' and sisters' ministry work in the church.

You and I are not always right about what we say and do in the church.

The greatest pastor in the church is not always right about every word he says and every deed he does.

People who love to point their finger at other people's mistakes with God's holy word are making a mistake in the presence of God.

People who love to point their finger at other people's flaws with God's holy word are flawed in the presence of God.

People who love to point their finger at other people's bad choices with God's holy word make a bad choice for pointing their finger in the presence of God.

People who point their finger at other people's bad deeds with God's holy word do a bad deed by pointing their finger in the presence of God.

People who point their finger at other people's sins with God's holy word have sinned against God for pointing their finger in His presence.

God's holy word shows no special favors for anyone in this sinful world where we all are born in sin to have a sinful nature.

Only Jesus Christ, our Lord and Savior, is worthy to point His perfect finger at you and me, because Jesus is the word of God that was made flash to live with sinners and to save sinners like you and me from our sins.

The Greatest Test Of Our Faith

The greatest test of our faith in Jesus Christ is to be willing to give up our life for Jesus' name sake.

Would we be willing to get our heads cut off of our bodies for Jesus' name sake?

Would we be willing to get burned up in hot flames of fire for Jesus' name sake?

Would we be willing to get shot up by a firing squad for Jesus' name sake?

Would we be willing to get thrown off a high mountain Cliff for Jesus name sake?

Would we be willing to get tied up with ropes and thrown in the ocean to drown for Jesus' name sake?

The greatest test of our faith in Jesus Christ is to be willing to give up our lives for Jesus' name sake.

Would we be willing to be thrown in a wood-chipper for Jesus' name sake?

Would we be willing to be thrown out of an airplane flying thousands of feet above the ground for Jesus' name sake?

Only Jesus knows if you and I have that kind of faith in Him to be willing to give up our lives for His holy name's sake.

Would we be willing to get rolled over by a speeding train for Jesus' name sake?

Would we be willing to be thrown in a lion's den for Jesus' name sake?

Would we be willing to be thrown in a pond full of crocodiles for Jesus' name sake?

Would we be willing to get thrown in a pit full of poisonous snakes for Jesus' name sake?

Only Jesus knows if you and I will pass the greatest test of our faith.

The Lord will not put on you and me more than we can bear.

Only the Lord knows if you and I can bear our greatest test of faith.

Would we be willing to get thrown in a pool of boiling oil for Jesus' name sake?

Would we be willing to get thrown in a gas chamber for Jesus' name sake?

Would we be willing to get thrown off a high bridge for Jesus' name sake?

Only the Lord knows who will be willing to give up their own life for His holy name's sake.

You and I just don't know if we will pass the greatest test of our faith in Him.

We Need To

We need to pray to the Lord and ask Him to help us do the things that we need to do.

It's truly the Lord who keeps us in our right minds and in good physical health to function normally in our lives.

We need to put our trust in the Lord day after day.

We need to love and obey the Lord day after day.

There are people who believe that they don't need to pray to the Lord and ask Him to help them do the things that they need to do.

There are people who believe that they made themselves to do things without the Lord's help.

There are people who believe that they can do anything on their own.

They won't acknowledge that it's the Lord who keeps breath in their bodies.

They won't acknowledge that it's the Lord who keeps strength in their bodies.

They won't acknowledge that it's the Lord who keeps them in their right minds from day to day.

We need to thank the Lord for helping us to make the right choices from day to day.

We need to give the Lord Jesus Christ the glory and the praise for helping us to accomplish things in our lives.

There are people who believe that they can accomplish things on their own without the help of the Lord.

It's truly the Lord who allows us to make some accomplishments in our lives.

We can make ourselves look like an island sitting all alone in the ocean waters if we believe that we don't need the Lord in our lives.

An island is all alone but just doesn't know it is all alone in the ocean waters.

There are people who don't realize that they are all alone for the devil to deceive them because of living their lives to exalt themselves.

We need to always exalt the Lord Jesus Christ who is worthy to be exalted forever and ever.

There are people who believe that they don't need the Lord and don't need to pray to the Lord because of believing that they are invincible.

We need the Lord, who is invincible, to give us eternal life in heaven when He comes back again.

Cities Are Made Up Of

Cities are made up of rich people, upper class people, middle class people, and poor people.

Cities are made up of educated people and uneducated people.

Cities are made up of young people, middle aged people, and old people.

Cities are made up of big people and small people.

Cities are made up of tall people and short people.

Cities are made up of wise people and foolish people.

Cities are made up of good people and bad people.

Cities are made up of healthy people and unhealthy people.

Cities are made up of happy people and sad people.

Cities are made up of successful people and unsuccessful people.

Cities are made up of talkative people and quiet people.

Cities are made up of attractive people and unattractive people.

There is a new Jerusalem holy city that will one day and be made up of holy and righteous people.

There is a new Jerusalem holy city that will one day be made up of sinless people.

There is a new Jerusalem holy city that will one day be made up of immortal people who will live forever and ever with Jesus Christ.

Jesus Christ is building that new Jerusalem holy city for Christian people like you and me to one day live in with Him.

Cities are made up of so many people living together, whether being good or bad.

The new Jerusalem holy city is the only city that Jesus can build so perfectly.

Jesus is building streets made of pure gold.

There will be no thieves in the new Jerusalem holy city to steal the golden streets and the twelve gates of pearls.

If there were streets of gold in this sinful world, many people would steal and kill to get them.

The cities in this world are filled with imperfect people.

The new Jerusalem holy city will be filled with perfect people.

The cities in this world are filled with so much sin.

The new Jerusalem holy city will be filled with the glory of God.
The cities in this world are made up of so many selfish people.

The new Jerusalem holy city will be made up of nothing but selfless people.

Don't Get Our Way

When we church folks don't get our way, it's not good for us to use God's word against people.

When we church folks don't get our way with one another, it's not good for us to cause one another to look bad.

It's so easy to want to get back at people if they don't do what we want them to do.

Our motives must be pure in what we do for the Lord.

If our motives are to do good things to make ourselves look good before people, then we will get upset with others if they don't support us.

We Christians can be quick to point our fingers at one another if we can't get our way, and we can be quick to use God's holy word against each other.

When we do this, we are not being like Jesus Christ whose goodness leads us to repent.

Our fingers pointing at one another's sins will not lead us to repent of our sins that we all do have.

We can have good intentions for doing good things, but if all of our brothers and sisters don't get on board, we don't have the right to believe that they are lost in their sins and will go to hell.

Only a fool has that mentality when not getting his or her way with people.

God loves everyone and God sufferings long with everyone.

You and I can get impatient with one another if we can't get our way.

If I was the only way that you could get to heaven and you were the only way that I could get to heaven, then we wouldn't get there because of the favoritism that we can show even in the church.

The people who we get our way with would be the ones we want to put in heaven.

The people who we don't get our way with, we would want them to go to hell.

Jesus Christ the Lord is not like that at all.

Especially we brothers and sisters in the Lord must know that God's way of doing things is higher than our way of doing things.

Our ways of doing things can be questioned if we are quick to use God's word against people for not getting our way.

Loves Everybody the Same

The Lord loves everybody the same.

You and I must love everybody the same, no matter what the color of their skin is.

The Lord doesn't love the president more than He loves the trash man.

The Lord doesn't love an aircraft pilot more than He loves a newspaper carrier.

The Lord doesn't love a scientist more than He loves a construction worker.

The Lord loves everybody the same.

You and I can fall short of loving everybody the same.

The Lord doesn't love a movie star more than He loves a shoemaker.

The Lord doesn't love a senator more than He loves a salesperson.

The Lord doesn't love an educated man more than He loves an uneducated man.

The Lord doesn't love a businessman more than He loves a prisoner.

The Lord loves everybody the same, every day.

The Lord sees no big you and little me in His loving eyesight.

To Him, no one is better than anyone else.

Many people in this world will love some people more than they love other people.

Many people in the church will love some people more than they love other people.

It's easy to love those who love us.

It's not easy to love those who don't love us.

Many people will love those who are living in a big beautiful house.

Many people will not love those who are homeless.

Many people will love those who are driving a beautiful, expensive car.

Many people will not love those who don't have a vehicle.

The Lord loves everybody the same.

Many people will love those who are sane.

Many people will not love those who are insane.

Many people will love those who look good.

Many people will not love those who don't look good.

The Lord loves everybody the same.

The Lord doesn't love a beautiful woman more than He loves an unattractive woman.

The Lord doesn't love a strong man more than He loves a weak man.

The Lord doesn't love a successful person more than He loves a failure.

The Lord loves everybody the same.

The Lord gave up His life on the cross where He shed His blood for everybody, great and small.

If You Think on the Lord

If you think on the Lord, He will give you peace of mind.

If you think on the things in this world, it can stress you out.

If you think on the Lord, He will lift you up out of your worries.

If you think on the things in this world, it can make you depressed.

If you think on the Lord, He will take away your fears.

If you think on the things in this world, it can discourage you.

If you think on the Lord, He will help you to go the extra mile.

If you think on the things in this world, it can cause you to give up on living.

If you think on the Lord, He will open your mind to spiritual things.

If you think on the things in this world, it can trouble your mind.

If you think on the Lord, He will comfort you to trust Him.

If you think on the things in this world, it can cause you to feel so uncomfortable, especially about your future.

If you think on the Lord, He will make you content with the things that you have.

If you think on the things in this world, it can make you to be so dissatisfied with the things that you have.

If you think on the Lord, He will never make you regret it.

If you think on the things in this world, it can make you regret thinking about worldly things.

If you think on the Lord, He will take your mind to heavenly places.

If you think on the things in this world, it can take your mind to some horrible places.

If you think on the Lord, He can give you hope.

If you think on the things in this world, it can cause you to have no hope.

If you think on the Lord, He will lead and guide you to make the right choices.

If you think on the things in this world, it can cause you to make the wrong choices.

If you think on the Lord, He will never disappoint you.

If you think on the things in this world, it can disappoint you.

If you think on the Lord, He will never let you down.

If you think on the things in this world, it can let you down.

That I Know

I am so glad, my Lord Jesus Christ, that I know to believe in You and be saved.

I am so joyful, my Lord Jesus Christ, that I know to worship You in spirit and truth.

I am so happy, my Lord Jesus Christ, that I know to deny myself and pick up my cross and follow you.

I am so grateful, my Lord Jesus Christ, that I know to put my trust in You.

I am so honored, my Lord Jesus Christ, that I know to give You all the glory and praise.

I am so sure, my Lord Jesus Christ, that I know to live my life doing Your holy will.

I am so hopeful, my Lord Jesus Christ, that I know you will never leave me or forsake me.

I am so very aware, my Lord Jesus Christ, that I know You will never fail me.

My Lord and Savior Jesus Christ, it is so good to know that You will forgive me of my sins if I confess and repent of my sins unto You.

My Lord and Savior Jesus Christ, it is so great to know that You will cleanse me of my sins through Your precious blood that You shed on the cross for my sins.

I am so pleased, my Lord Jesus Christ, that I know to read Your holy word for myself.

I am so satisfied, my Lord Jesus Christ, that I know that You will give me the victory to overcome the world ways of living.

Will Not Go to Heaven

Every Pope will not go to heaven.

Every pastor will not go to heaven.

Every Bishop will not go to heaven.

Every elder will not go to heaven.

Every deacon will not go to heaven.

Every usher will not go to heaven.

Every deaconess will not go to heaven.

Every Bible school teacher will not go to heaven.

Every church member will not go to heaven.

Everyone in the church doesn't always have good motives.

Everyone in the church doesn't always have good intentions.

Everyone in the church doesn't always love all of their brothers and sisters.

Everyone in the church doesn't always respect all of their brothers and sisters.

Everyone in the church will not go to heaven.

Everyone in the church doesn't always mean all of their brothers and sisters good will.

Everyone in the church doesn't love Jesus Christ.

Everyone in the church isn't saved in Jesus Christ.

Everyone in the church is not born again.

Everyone in the church is not humble unto the Lord Jesus Christ.

Everyone in the church doesn't always confess and repent of their sins.

Everyone in the church will not always hold grudges.

Everyone in the church will not go to heaven.

Everyone in the church will not have faith in Jesus Christ.

Everyone in the church will not keep God's commandments.

Everyone in the church doesn't always have a relationship with Jesus Christ.

Everyone in the church doesn't care about all of their brothers and sisters making it to heaven.

Everyone in the church isn't living a sermon.

Close His Probation on this World

The Lord will one day close His probation on this world.

Many church folks will not be anchored in the Lord.

Many church folks will not be sealed in the Lord.

Many church folks will not be saved in the Lord.

The Lord will one day close His probation on this world.

Many church folks are worshiping the things in this world.

Many church folks are putting their trust in themselves and believe that they can save themselves and enter into heaven one day.

Many church folks are putting their trust in the temporary things in this world.

The Lord will one day close probation on this world.

When that will be, we just don't know.

Many church folks are compromising with the traditions of this world.

Many church folks are divided in the church.

Many church folks have cliques in the church.

The Lord will one day close probation on this world.

Many church folks are not standing up for equality.

Many church folks are not standing up for justice.

Many church folks are not standing up for the truth of God's holy word.

The Lord will one day close probation on this world.

Many church folks have bad motives behind the good things they do.

Many church folks will throw indirect words at their brothers and sisters in the church to make them look bad so that they can make themselves look good and right.

The Lord will one day close probation on this world.

Many church folks are spiritually sleeping in the church.

Many church folks are willfully sinning against the Lord.

Many church folks believe that they deserve to make it to heaven.

The Lord will one day close probation on this world.

Many church folks will despise you and me for telling them the truth about themselves.

The Lord will one day close probation on this world where pretend Christians will be judged the hardest like the angels that fell from heaven.

I Want to do Your Will, O Lord

I want to do Your will, O Lord.

Your will is perfect.

My will is so flawed.

I want to do Your will, O Lord.

Your will is holy.

My will is so defected.

I want to do Your will, O Lord.

Your will is righteous.

My will can do wrong things.

I want to do Your will, O Lord.

Your will is everlasting love.

My will can fall short of loving You and my neighbors.

I want to do Your will, O Lord.

Your will is always peaceful.

My will can give me some trouble.

I want to do Your will, O Lord.

Your will is truthful every day.

My will can lie to me every day.

Will Hurt Our Hearts

When a loved one dies, it will hurt our hearts and we will grieve.

The pain will never go away, but it will ease up as time goes on.

As our pets grow old, it can hurt our hearts because we know even our pets will one day die.

Love is a very powerful thing that brings out the best in anyone's life.

Our hearts wouldn't hurt if we didn't love our loved ones and if we didn't love our pets.

Our hearts will hurt when a loved one dies.

Our hearts will hurt when our pets die.

It won't hurt our hearts to grieve.

Our hearts will hurt because of the close connection that we had with our loved ones.

Our hearts will hurt because of the close connection that we had with our pets.

People will die and animals will die, if we have no close connection with them then we won't feel any hurt, but that doesn't mean we don't care.

Our hearts will hurt when those who we love go through some hardships, because we don't want to see them suffer — we don't even want to see our pets suffer from sadness.

It should hurt our hearts knowing that Jesus Christ suffered on the cross to save us from our sins.

He shed His blood and died for us to be saved in Him.

Medicine Can't Cure the Sin-Sick Soul

Medicine can't cure the sin-sick soul.

Only Jesus Christ can cure the sin-sick soul.

Medicine can't cure bad motives.

Medicine can't cure bad intentions.

Medicine can't cure bad words.

Medicine can't cure flaws.

Medicine can't cure bad habits.

Only Jesus Christ can cure the sin-sick soul.

Medicine can't cure wrong-doings.

Medicine can't cure bad thoughts.

Medicine can't cure ill feelings.

Medicine can't cure selfishness.

Only Jesus Christ can cure the sin-sick soul.

Medicine can't cure mistakes.

Medicine can't cure the sinful nature.

Only Jesus Christ, our Lord and Savior, can cure our sin-sick souls through His precious blood that was shed on the cross for our sins.

Medicine can't cure the sin-sick soul.

Medicine will never be strong enough to cure this sin-sick soul.

Medicine can't cure anyone from sinning against the Lord.

Medicine can't cure anyone from breaking God's commandments.

The very best medicine can't stop anyone from saying anything wrong and doing anything wrong.

Only Jesus can cure the sin-sick soul.

No One is More

No one is more genius than the truth.

No one is more brilliant than the truth.

No one is smarter than the truth.

No one is more wise than the truth.

No one is more beautiful than the truth.

No one is more real than the truth.

No one is more sure than the truth.

No one is more brave than the truth.

No one is more dependable than the truth.

No one is more loving than the truth.

No one is more trustworthy then the truth.

No one is more fair than the truth.

No one is more stable than the truth.

The only way to worship God is in spirit and in truth.

Jesus Christ, our Lord and Savior, is the truth.

You Can Always Talk to Jesus

If you feel depressed, you can always talk to Jesus, who can take your depression away if you ask Him to and believe that He can by faith.

If you feel like that no one loves you, then you can always talk to Jesus, who loves you more than you will ever know.

Jesus is very real and will always talk to you about anything that is heavy on your mind.

If you and I talk to Jesus about our struggles and hardships, He will give us strength to deal with them.

You and I can always talk to Jesus, who is the best one to always talk to.

Jesus fully understands and feels our pain, and He will take it away from us if we trust Him to do that.

Jesus always knows how we truly feel.

Jesus always knows what we can bear and what we can't bear.

If you truly believe in Jesus, you will experience His power to make you strong when you feel weak with fear and depression.

You and I can always talk to Jesus at any time of the day and night.

Jesus is always with us to strengthen us.

We are Not Going Anywhere

We black people are not going anywhere when we also have made this nation great.

Today, we black people not only belong here in America, we belong here in this whole world that God created us in to live with every other race, creed and culture of people.

Our black lives matter to God, who created us to be distinct from every other race of people.

Our black distinction is of very good use to God every day that we are not going anywhere away from this world.

The world is also our world for us black people to enjoy living in, and prejudice and oppression can't take our joy away.

We are like the oceans that will not go anywhere.

We are like the sky that will not go anywhere.

We are like the ground that will not go anywhere.

We are like the universe that will not go anywhere.

We black people are here to stay until Jesus Christ comes back again to also take many of us black people back to heaven with Him.

Time has always been on our side to help us black people immigrate all over this world.

Time was on our ancestors' side to help them claim their presence for being here in this world.

Most of all, God has always been on our side to bring us black people this far for us to know that we are not going anywhere from making good contributions to this world.

Many of us black people contribute our talents and skills to this world.

Many of us black people contribute our time and peace to this world.

Many of us black people contribute our love and intelligence to this world.

Many of us black people contribute our education and faith in God to this world.

We black people are not going anywhere when many of us black people are hard-working people and getting less pay.

Many of us black people have a fear for God.

We black people are not going anywhere away from this world.

We are like the air that will not go away.

This world will one day come to an end and go down into fire and brimstone, when many of us black people will also be in the new Jerusalem Holy City with Jesus Christ and every other race of people who are saved in Jesus Christ.

All of us saved black people will not go anywhere away from the new heaven and new earth that Jesus will create for all of the saints.

We black people are not going anywhere in a world of injustice toward us.

We black people are not going anywhere in a world of inequality toward us. We are not going anywhere in a world of prejudice toward us.

We are not going anywhere in a world of oppression toward us.

We are not going anywhere in a world of discrimination toward us.

We are not going anywhere in a world of hatred toward us.

We black people were destined by God to live in this world.

Many of us black people are not going anywhere away from putting in our efforts to make this world a better place for everybody to live in.

Many of us black people are not going anywhere away from loving our neighbors in every race, creed and culture of people.

We black people are here to stay in this world for as long as we exist.

The sand will run out of an hourglass, but we black people are not going anywhere away from this world.

Water will run down a drain, but we black people are not going anywhere away from this world.

A tornado will blow a house down, but we black people are not going anywhere away from this world.

Prejudice will not cause us to go anywhere away from this world.

Injustice will not cause us to go anywhere away from this world.

Discrimination will not cause us to go anywhere away from this world.

Inequality will not cause us to go anywhere away from this world.

Hatred will not cause us to go anywhere away from this world.

Oppression will not cause us to go anywhere away from this world.

Stereotyping will not cause us to go anywhere away from this world.

God created us black people to live in this world with every other race of people.

We black people are not going anywhere away from this world that has plenty of space for us black people to live in.

We black people are not going anywhere away from ignorance.

The sun will rise and set on us black people.

The sun will not move anywhere away from us all day long.

The moonlight will glow down on us black people.

The moonlight will not move anywhere away from us all night long.

The stars will sparkle down on us black people.

The stars will not move anywhere away from us all night long.

Nature doesn't want us black people to go anywhere away from this world.

Many racist people will move far away from us black people, if they don't want to live next to us black people.

Many of us black people still love them, but we will not accept their prejudices against us.

If the sun stops shining, we are not going anywhere away from this world.

If the moonlight stops glowing, we are not going anywhere away from this world.

If the stars stop sparkling, we are not going anywhere away from this world.

If the rivers stop running into the oceans, we are not going anywhere away from this world.

If all the harvested crops dry up, we are not going anywhere away from this world.

Evolution can spread like the Corona virus, but we black people are not going anywhere away from this world.

This world is also our world to live in until Jesus Christ comes back again.

This great nation is also our nation to live in until Jesus Christ comes back again.

Many of us black people love the color of our skin.

If some black people don't like the way they look, then they don't like the way that God created them to look.

God didn't make any mistakes when He created us black people.

Racist people believe that we black people weren't created in the image of God.

God hates prejudice, whether its many white people being prejudiced against black people or whether it's many black people being prejudiced against white people.

There is nothing good about being prejudiced against anyone.

We black people will always exist and will not go anywhere away from this world of many prejudiced people who can't get rid of us black people, because God won't allow them to succeed in doing that.

www.ingramcontent.com/pod-product-compliance
Lightning Source LLC
Chambersburg PA
CBHW070110080526
44586CB00013B/1255